DISTANT MEMORIES

RONALD SIEBERT

Copyright © *Ronald Siebert,* 2025
All rights reserved.

No part of this publication may be reproduced, stored in a retrieval system, or transmitted in any form or by any means—electronic, mechanical, photocopying, recording, or otherwise—without the prior written permission of the author, except for brief quotations used in reviews or scholarly works.

TABLE OF CONTENTS

Chapter 1 1
Chapter 2 5
Chapter 3 9
Chapter 4 14
Chapter 5 18
Chapter 6 21
Chapter 7 25
Chapter 8 31
Chapter 9 35
Chapter 10 40
Chapter 11 46
Chapter 12 51
Chapter 13 56
Chapter 14 60
Chapter 15 66
Chapter 16 72
Chapter 17 77
Chapter 18 83
Chapter 19 85
Chapter 20 89
Chapter 21 92
Chapter 22 98
Chapter 23 102
Chapter 24 106
Chapter 25 114
Chapter 26 119
Chapter 27 124

Chapter 28 128
Chapter 29 133
Chapter 30 138
Chapter 31 141
Chapter 32 146
Chapter 33 149
Chapter 34 152
Chapter 35 157
Chapter 36 163
Chapter 37 169
Chapter 38 172
Chapter 39 174
Chapter 40 176
Chapter 41 182
Chapter 42 188
Chapter 43 192
Chapter 44 195
Chapter 45 199
Chapter 46 202
Chapter 47 205
Chapter 48 211
Chapter 49 219
Chapter 50 222
Chapter 51 226
Chapter 52 233
Chapter 53 238
Chapter 54 244
Chapter 55 249
Chapter 56 252
Chapter 57 257

Chapter 58 264
Chapter 59 269
Chapter 60 272
Chapter 61 276
Chapter 62 281

CHAPTER 1

An old dilapidated shack, worn gray from years of abuse, sits deep within overgrown trees and bushes. At first glance, anyone would think the building abandoned. Trash and old toys littering the area were long ago hidden by weeds that had grown nearly as high as the cracked and broken windows. In the rear of the shack, an old rusted junk car lay scattered around the area, where at one time a garage used to be. Remains of the garage lay crumpled behind the shack.

The shack itself was void of paint. With most of its shingles missing, gaping holes in the roof allowed rainwater to flow freely into the building. All the windows were broken or cracked. The few remaining shards of glass were caked with mud and grime, allowing critters and dampness inside.

In the front of the shack, a small crumbling porch, with its one screen door, held up by one rusty hinge, sagged to one side, useless. At night, the only sign of life in the shack is a small light lit in one of the back windows.

Inside the shack were four small rooms. All the rooms were worn, dingy, and smelled of smoke and booze. No pictures hang on the bare walls. None of the rooms has lamps, except the larger of the two bedrooms, where Karen slept.

In the filthy living room stands a broken end table on three legs. A soiled stack of old magazines piled under one corner of that table, provided the fourth leg. An old shabby chair, with its stuffing half removed, sat haphazardly near the dilapidated table, shoved tightly into one corner of the tiny room.

Lying around the chair and table were many broken and empty bottles of different kinds of whiskey and wine. Remnants of spilled liquid soiled the shaggy rug beneath the table and chair. Unpleasant aromas of old booze and urine stung the nostrils of anyone entering the room.

The smaller of the two bedrooms, the cleanest room in the shack, belongs to Karen's two children. One tiny double bed, always neatly made, filled the room. One small closet in the room housed old, torn pants and shabby dresses. A tiny chest, with its top broken and removed, sat beneath the clothes inside the closet. Inside the chest are the rest of the clothes, belonging to the two children who occupy the room.

The largest bedroom belonged to their mother, Karen, where she entertains her nightly male friends.

At one time, Karen had been a tall, beautiful blonde woman, with flowing curves supplementing a voluptuous body. Long blond hair hung in waves just below her shoulders. A wave of that beautiful hair, when clean and silky, used to hang over her left shoulder, unable to cover her large breast. Her face, long and narrow, had a small cleft on her chin. Soft blue eyes, with a long, narrow nose and soft red lips, the lower lip always pouting, begged to be kissed.

In her younger years, Karen had won many beauty contests, not only with her beautiful face, but also with her tall, well-proportioned body. Her then slender body, with large soft breasts, slender waist, rounded hips, and long muscular legs, turned many eyes as she passed by.

Even now, in her later years, after heavy drug and alcohol abuse, Karen still had no trouble finding a man to sleep with. Some of the men paid her for her favors, while others fed her kids, and kept her in booze and drugs.

The fourth room, a tiny kitchen, is infested with cockroaches. The kitchen was by far the filthiest room in the shack, with old food, papers, and dirty dishes littering the small table and counter. Rotten food and dried muck, tracked in and never cleaned, caked the floor. Even the thousands of cockroaches, living in the filth, seemed unafraid of intruders. The only time the roaches scurry, into any hole available, would be when the item they occupied was moved.

Even though Karen still loved her two children, she was now unable to show it. Eighteen-year-old Ralph, the oldest and a senior in high school, still carried high grades and still found time for school activities. Even when Ralph participated, he always had time to care for his twelve-year-old sister Vanessa.

Vanessa, a seventh grader, also carried good grades. Vanessa is the only person in Ralph's life who gives him the love and comfort he needs to sustain. Because of her love and devotion, Ralph makes sure to return what she gives him tenfold.

On days when Ralph was occupied with school activities, Vanessa would be home washing clothes and cooking supper. She wanted Ralph to eat a good meal when he got home. At this time in their young lives, Ralph has made it a point to become the overseer of his younger sister.

Life had not always been bad for Ralph. Thirteen years ago, when Ralph was five, he was a happy, content child, living in a nice, clean home. The home was in the better part of town, where he was loved and adored by both parents. Both his mother and father encouraged Ralph to do school and church activities by supporting him and being with him whenever they could. Because of the support and knowledge he had received, Ralph became confident, knowing he could do anything he set his mind to do.

Someday, Ralph thought, he was going to be rich, so he could take care of his family, as they had taken care of him. He hoped that one day, when he was old enough to date, he'd be able to take care of a good woman like his mom, marry her, and have children. But, before Ralph could even think of marriage, he had to grow up, go to college, and get a better education.

The one thing Ralph knew he didn't want was to be a cop like his father. His father spent too much time away from home. Too many times, Ralph could hear his mother crying from loneliness and the fear that her husband might be killed doing his job. Ralph didn't understand why his mother always put up with the many nights and days his dad never came home.

When his dad was home, it was as if his father was never gone, and they would be like a normal family. He could see the love his mother needed in her face. Ralph hoped someday, his parents would give him a brother, or a sister, before it was too late.

A brother would be nice, he thought. He would have someone to play with when it was storming out. Loneliness always set in when it stormed.

If he had a little sister, his mom and dad would devote all their time to her. Like so many of his friends, their sister always ran to their mom and dad and told on them. He would rather have a brother.

CHAPTER 2

Ralph's father, Roy Anderson, had been a detective on the city police force. His mother Karen worked for the State as a consultant.

Roy Anderson met Karen Olson in their senior year of college. When they first met, they didn't like each other. Karen used to say Roy had an ego bigger than both of them put together.

Often thrown together, they did their best to ignore each other. Finally, fate had it that they met in most areas on the campus: the library, math, English, and gym.

For them, gym was modern dancing. For some reason, becoming partners was inevitable. As partners, they began to see each other differently and started dating. As time passed, falling in love was inevitable too. They married soon after graduation. Both were twenty-two.

Moving to the city gave them opportunities for better jobs with the state. Roy became a police officer, Karen a secretary. Working hard at their professions paid off. Roy advanced to Lieutenant, while Karen became a consultant for the state. With the money they had saved over the years, they were able to buy a large ranch-style home on the outskirts of the city. For them, it was a perfect place to live and raise a family.

Established in the workforce, they decided to have a child. After eight happy years of marriage, Ralph was born. They tried having another child soon after, but for some reason Karen couldn't conceive again.

Happily married for thirteen years, tragedy hit when, at the age of thirty-five, Roy became a casualty while on a stakeout. A drug lord, Roy, had been casing, had gotten away with the crime because of a lack of evidence.

Devastated from the loss of her love, thirty-five-year-old Karen lapsed into depression. She began drinking, lightly at first. Then day by day, week by week, her drinking became heavier. It wasn't long before Karen began staying out until all hours of the night.

Ralph, only five felt the blow harder than his mother. Ralph was now suddenly left to his own needs. One year after Roy died, Karen gave birth to a girl she named Vanessa. Having slept with too many men, in too short a time, Karen had no idea which of the men was Vanessa's father.

The day after Vanessa's first birthday, Karen lost her job. Bad habits, and with a growing bad reputation, Karen couldn't find another job. Little by little, Karen spent all her savings on booze and drugs. Finally, all Karen was left with was the small retirement Roy had left her. Unable to keep the house, she sold it.

Relying on one of her steady customers for support, Karen moved with what was left of her family into a small shack in the outskirts of the town. Her bouts with liquor and men became habitual. It was a habit she could not and did not want to break. After a while, the types of men she slept with didn't matter. As long as they fed her kids, and kept her in booze and drugs, she was content.

With no maintenance, the shack began to fall apart. Even as much as Ralph loved his mother, he began to distance himself from her. The only thing Karen liked about Ralph was the way he took care of his squalling brat sister, the daughter she never wanted. To have a little privacy for herself, Karen made her children sleep together, in the smallest bedroom, in a small double bed.

Ralph was ten, six years older than his sister Vanessa. Many nights, through the first three years, Vanessa would wake Ralph kicking and crying, because she had wet the bed, or was hungry. At first, Ralph tried to ignore his baby sister, hoping his mother would hear her and come to her aid. When Ralph finally realized, his mother was too drunk or busy with her boyfriends to tend to her daughter, Ralph decided to take care of her himself.

After a while, Ralph became used to helping Vanessa. He began to enjoy watching her. She was growing into a cute little girl. Feeling sorry for his sister, for the neglect their mother gave them, Ralph began hating his mother. Ralph found it easier and faster to do everything for his sister himself.

Pity for Vanessa soon turned to love. She was the love Ralph so sorely needed in his life. To his amazement, his love and devotion to Vanessa were returned to him tenfold. It was Ralph who potty trained his sister, bathed her, read stories to her, and held her at night when she was frightened.

When Vanessa turned five, Ralph took her to school, enrolled her in classes, and helped her with her homework. Even with all his chores at home, Ralph still found time for school activities. Whenever Ralph had a game, Vanessa would go with him to cheer him on. At first, the other kids teased Ralph about his young girlfriend. Being smart, Ralph ignored the jaunts. Eventually, they found their taunting couldn't intimidate him. Becoming his friends, they stopped their taunting.

When Ralph turned fifteen, he began to learn about cars from a friend who owned a garage near the junk yard. This friend worked out of his own home. Skipping school one day, for a few hours, Ralph had his friend and helped him move the rusted junk car from his backyard to his friend's garage across town.

To work on his car, Ralph had to leave Vanessa on her own a few hours, a couple of nights a week. Any time Ralph had the time and money for the parts, his friend would help him restore the old Chevy. Parts were easy to find. Paying for them was difficult. Ralph stored his car in a garage at the junkyard.

This old car needed a couple of coats of paint, Ralph thought one day. When his car was nearly finished, Ralph thought about giving it a couple of coats of paint. Ralph had only one objective, and that was to get Vanessa away from this town. Before going, he would get his car painted.

"Vanessa, I have to go out for a while. Will you be all right?" Ralph asked.

"Sure, I'll wash clothes and go to bed early."

"I should wash clothes too."

"Just give me your clothes, I'll do them with mine," she said.

"Thanks, Vanessa, I love you."

"I love you too, Ralph."

For an eight-year-old, Vanessa was quite self-sufficient. All her thanks belonged to her brother for his time and devotion he gave her. As the years passed, their love and devotion for each other grew.

Now eighteen, Ralph was ready to graduate. He could hardly wait to take Vanessa away from this pigpen. Ralph had worked hard to get the car ready and to have enough money saved to make the run. What happened one night not only made Ralph worry about his sister; he was afraid it could happen again when he wasn't home. Another worry was being found once he got them away.

CHAPTER 3

One night, a week before graduation, Vanessa lay close to Ralph in bed, to stay warm. Nearly asleep, Ralph heard someone open the bedroom door. Being a light sleeper, just the sound of the door opening awakened Ralph. Opening his eyes, a slit, Ralph didn't move. Pretending to be asleep, hoping whoever was in the room could not tell he was being watched and leave.

A sliver of light shone on the intruder's face. Not knowing the person entering their bedroom, Ralph waited. Every muscle in his body tensed. As the shadow moved closer to his sister's side of the bed, Ralph quickly made his move. Before the assailant could react, Ralph sprang to his feet, pushing the man against the wall.

"Hey, what the hell?" the man said.

The man's words uttered were slurred. Ralph knew the man was mean drunk.

"What do you want?" Ralph asked, knowing what the man was after.

"None of your fucking business, sonny," the man told Ralph.

As the drunk slowly moved toward the bed, Ralph away, Ralph reacted quickly. Punching the man in the stomach, Ralph waited to see the man's reaction. The punch was heavy and solid. Taking the wind out of the man's lungs, the man doubled over. A rancid smell of vomit permeated the room.

For a moment, as the man bent over spewing a mixture of food and booze, Ralph waited. Done spewing, the man wiped his mouth and glared at Ralph. Seeing the mess covering the floor and part of the bed, Ralph didn't give the guy a chance to recover. Quickly lifting his knee, Ralph hit the man in the face. Sounds of bones crunching filled the room. His knee connected with the man's nose. Blood and snot spewed on Ralph's undershirt and briefs.

With the force of the blow from Ralph's knee, the man's head slammed back into the wall, with a shattering force. The force of the man's head hitting the wall put a hole in the plaster. Any normal man would have been down for the count. Ralph couldn't count the times he had to fight off his mother's drunken slobs.

Most of the men would quickly retreat before any punches were thrown. Others would leave after a single punch. Never had Ralph had to hurt a man as he had hurt this one. Some of the men Ralph had to fight off were big men, as this man was, but none of them were ever this mean.

Standing his ground over the man lying against the wall, he waited for the man to move. Blood flowed freely from the man's broken nose, and oozed from his split lips. With blood dribbling from the corners of his mouth, the man staggered to his feet again. Standing and weaving, the man spoke, causing fresh blood to splatter on the shattered wall behind him.

"Get the hell out of my way, kid," the man said.

Trying to push Ralph aside again, Ralph had to hit him again, this time in the face with his fist. Again, blood and mucus flew around the room. The man sank to his knees. The punch had hurt Ralph's hand, yet it still didn't stop the man.

"Damn," he said, grabbing his flattened and bloody nose.

Getting up from the floor, the huge man came toward Ralph again saying, "I'm going to kill you for this."

Frightened, Ralph knew he had a huge problem coming at him. This man was definitely not going down easy. Reaching behind him, Ralph tightly clutched the baseball bat lying against the wall, by the bed.

The man moved slowly toward him.

Waiting until the man was enough to smell booze and blood, Ralph could see hatred in the man's eyes. His arms were outstretched as he stumbled toward Ralph. With no choice, Ralph swung the bat at the man's knees. The blow connected with the man's kneecap. With an eerie howl of a wounded animal, the man fell to his back. Deep howls of pain emitted from the man's throat.

Hearing the breaking of bones, as the bat connected with the man's kneecaps, Ralph felt sick. Yet to Ralph's despair, the man wasn't done. The man was so drunk and strong, the man's mind overrode the sheer pain.

Reaching up to grab Ralph by the ankle, Ralph was now feeling fear. With panic setting in, Ralph swung the bat again. This time Ralph aimed at the ribs just below the outstretched arms of the man. Again, the sounds of bone breaking filled the room.

Without another word, the man rolled into the fetal position. Ralph waited a few moments to be sure the man was down for good. He had to be sure the man wouldn't get up again. Moments passed, and the man remained down. Knowing the fight was over, Ralph finally let out a sigh of relief.

Staring into the darkness, Ralph felt exhausted. A deep fear quickly grew inside Ralph. At that moment, he knew he had to get Vanessa away, far away, and it had to be soon.

The scuffle, grunts, and screams of pain made Vanessa huddle against the wall in utter terror. Overcome with fear for her brother, Vanessa sobbed. Wrapping her arms tightly around her tiny body, she rocked back and forth.

Seeing with her own eyes that the man was down for good, Vanessa scampered from the bed. Her eyes were as big as saucers. Grabbing one of the man's legs, Ralph said, "Help me, Vanessa."

Quickly grabbing the man's other leg, Vanessa helped her brother drag the man out of their bedroom. They dragged the man down the hall and into their mother's bedroom. The man was so big and heavy, the exertion put a lot of strain on Vanessa's small frame. Finally managing to get the man into their mother's room, they left him crumpled and bleeding on the floor next to their mother's bed.

Glancing at the bed, Ralph saw his mother's pitiful naked body lying before them. Passed out drunk, her once beautiful body was now in ruin. Lying with her arms and legs spread wide, sperm dripped from her red and swollen vagina. As drunk as their mother was, she never even heard any noise coming from the other room. At that moment, Ralph had no pity for his mother, only disgust.

With the man, battered and bleeding, lying on the cold, damp floor beside his mother's bed, Ralph and Vanessa left the room. They didn't bother covering their mother's naked body.

Now, Ralph was really frightened. He knew that some night, in the near future, one of the men, when sober enough, would return to overtake him. If that were to happen, neither he nor Vanessa would stand a chance of getting away. Lying in each other's arms, neither of them slept very much the rest of the night.

In the morning, as the sun began to rise, Ralph got out of bed, allowing his sister to sleep a little longer. Quietly and tentatively, expecting trouble, Ralph moved toward his mother's room. Seeing the door wide open, he was almost afraid to look inside. Swallowing his fear, Ralph peeked around the corner.

Except for his mother, the room was empty. Sometime in the night, the man, even with the pain he had to be feeling, had gotten up and left the shack. As badly beaten as the man was, he had to have help.

That same day, with hopes of buying time until graduation was over, Ralph fixed the door with new locks and bolts to ensure added safety. Now, no one would be able to get into the room again without getting hurt in the process.

For Ralph and Vanessa, nights became a difficult time to get proper rest. Restless with worry, they tossed and turned, leaving the sheets sodden with sweat. Other times, while asleep, Vanessa would press her tiny body into his, for warmth and comfort.

Immediately, Ralph would awaken. The feel of her warm body pressing against him was something he would never get used to. He was at the age of wanting and needing a woman, but Vanessa was his sister. Besides being too young, Vanessa wasn't the kind of woman he wanted or needed. Even if she could give him what he needed, he didn't want that from her.

Soon, Ralph began to realize, Vanessa received comfort from him by snuggling as close to him as she could. Once the panic of his need passed, instead of pushing her away, he would smile, wrap his arm around her sleeping body, and pull her closer to him. Every time, he embraced her, she would instinctively grab his arm, pinning it tightly against her tiny body.

There were nights when Vanessa would wiggle her little bottom against him as she snuggled in. The movement always gave him an erection. Knowing he shouldn't be having those feeling or thinking of things like that about Vanessa, he vowed to put a stop to it. However, because he didn't want to hurt her feelings, he didn't do anything about it. Besides becoming accustomed to her warmth and smell, Ralph liked the feel of her little body snuggling against him.

Each day brought them closer to the time for them to escape. The car was finished, waiting to be used. Since finishing the car, he has been able to save a little money. It wasn't much and it wouldn't get them very far, but he would just have to do the best he could.

Ralph knew he would graduate a couple of days before Vanessa got out for the summer, which was fine with him. Maybe he could earn a little more money helping his buddy around the garage.

CHAPTER 4

Summer was here. Ralph had just graduated from high school the week before.

His mother never knew he had graduated. Ralph had made it a point to tell her. A dozen times, he told her when and where the graduation would be. As he expected, she didn't make an appearance. The only person who stood by him was Vanessa, skinny, adorable, Vanessa. How he loved his sister.

Two days later, Vanessa graduated from the seventh grade. Their mother didn't bother going to her reception either. As usual, it was Ralph who stood by her. Totally discussed with his mother, one night while their mother was out with one of her many men, Ralph decided it was time to leave.

Going to his friend's garage, where he had his car stored, Ralph drove home. Parking behind the shack where no one would see the car, as quietly and quickly as he could, Ralph entered the house. He had to get Vanessa away before their mother came home. Finding her in her usual place, sitting on the bed, Ralph confronted her.

"Vanessa, let's get away from here," he said

"Where would we go?"

"Anywhere, away from here," he said

"How will we go?" she asked

"Remember the old junk car that used to be parked out back?"

"Yeah," she said.

"Well, I fixed it."

"Did you really?"

"Yeah, so do you want to go with me?" he asked.

"Of course, I do. But shouldn't we tell mom?"

"No, she might tell one of her boyfriends, and you know what would happen if they find us."

"You're right. Let's get out of here," she said.

Taking what clothes they had, they stuffed them into the trunk of the old rusty car. Taking a last look at what was their home for years, Ralph drove away from the shack to never look back. Neither Ralph nor Vanessa would really miss their mother, nor would they miss the sordid events that made them leave.

"We have to make one stop, before we leave for good."

"Why?" Vanessa asked.

"We need to look different that we do now. It is too obvious that you are too young to be on your own."

"You're eighteen," Vanessa said.

"Yes, but you definitely don't look old enough to be married."

"Married?"

"To make this work, we have to make people think we are married."

"That should be fun," Vanessa said.

A few minutes later, Ralph pulled into the garage where he had redone the car. Harvey, Ralph's friend, met them as Ralph drove into the yard.

"What's up, Ralph?"

"It's too late for a paint job, but can you help us with disguises?"

"Yeah, I think so," he said, "You and I are about the same size, and your sister and my sister could be twins."

After hugs goodbye, Harvey gave Ralph enough money to tide them over until he could find a job. Thirty minutes later, Ralph drove away forever. Vanessa, sitting close to her brother, looked four or five years older than her actual age. Ralph couldn't believe what a little makeup, a wig, and faults' tits could do to make a twelve-year-old girl look older.

"I'll pay you back someday, I promise," Ralph said, hugging his Friend.

"You don't have to pay me back," Harvey said, "Call it a gift to a cute married couple."

"Thanks, but I will pay you back."

"Whatever. Now get out of here before it's too late."

The car, an old rusty Chevrolet, ran smoothly and comfortably. As Ralph drove, Vanessa sat against the passenger's door looking out the window. She was looking at places she had never seen before, but had dreamed about, as the sights went by. It was so sad, Vanessa thought, and here she was, almost thirteen, and she had never been this far from home before.

They had been on the road for hours. Luck was still with them, or maybe their mother hadn't missed them yet. It was such a beautiful day outside that they rolled down the windows to let the fresh air in. With the windows down, feeling the wind blow through their hair relaxed them.

Soon, the sun began sinking behind the hills. Needing gas, Ralph pulled into the first gas station he came to. A young boy came out of the station to wait on them. The boy pumped the gas then checked the oil, before closing the hood. Feeling hungry, Ralph's first thought was about Vanessa. Because she never said anything about being hungry, he decided to wait until morning.

As tired as he felt, Ralph drove to a parking space behind the station and shut off the engine. Getting a couple of blankets from the trunk, he covered his sister, who was curled up in the front seat. Then curling up on the back seat, he quickly dropped off to sleep.

"Aren't we getting a room?" Vanessa asked.

"Not tonight, Vanessa. I don't want to take the chance of being caught, this close to home. Besides, we have to conserve our money until I can find a job."

"Does that mean I have to sleep alone every night?"

"Just tonight, tomorrow we will stop at a motel, I promise."

"Okay," she sighed, "Good night, Ralph."

Snuggling down under her blanket to try and keep warm, she closed her eyes.

"Goodnight, Vanessa. I love you."

"I love you too, Ralph," she told him.

In minutes, they fell into an exhausted sleep.

Chapter 5

"What do you suppose goes on over there?"

"Whatever it was, ain't anymore."

"That's for sure."

With the commotion going by, the people went back into their homes to forget anything had happened. The excitement was over. Now they could go back to doing what it was they were doing before the interruption.

The Bailey shack was the only place in that direction. Abandoned at one time, it was assumed local kids shared drunken and sexual parties without being bothered. As far as anyone in the small community knew, no one was living there and hadn't for some time. Thoughts were that some kids started the fire. Shutting out things that happen in the area was common practice.

About a half-mile up the road, emergency vehicles turned onto what seemed an unused road. Charred remains of an old shack, along with the area around it, were the only sight to be seen. Most of the property in that area for miles around was owned by the Bailey family.

In the beginning, an old logger lived there for years, with his wife and children. When the kids grew and moved away, it was just he and his wife. When the man's wife died, he then became a recluse. Finally, when the old man died, the surviving children inherited the farm. One of their sons, named Richard Bailey, controlled the property, using the property and the shack as a tax write-off. He refused to sell.

Little did anyone in the immediate area know, except those who frequented the place, Richard let Karen and her children stay on the shack rent-free out of pity. In return for the free rent, he had the use of her body anytime he wanted.

As the emergency vehicles neared the charred structure, they saw it was too late to save the building.

"I hope no one was in there," the assistant Fire Chief said to his superior.

"We'll know as soon as the police finish their investigation."

The blaze was now spreading to adjoining fields. If they didn't work fast, in moments the fire would be out of control.

"Get the men out in the field. We don't want this fire to get out of hand," the Chief said.

Quickly spreading their forces, the firefighters surrounded the spreading fires. Being only a grass fire, they soon got the fires under control. The shack was rubble. Full containment would not be far off. Nothing except the small shack, a few small bushes, and a few hundred yards of weeds that used to be in the vicinity had burned. The local Fire Department had responded quickly to the alarm set by the Emergency Fire Service tower.

After the Fire Department departed, the Police Arson Squad sifted through the rubble for the next two days. In the ashes, they found the remains of one body, charred beyond recognition.

An anonymous telephone call gave the police clues to who the body belonged. When forensics finished with what was left of the body, the police searched dental records using the tip from the telephone call. With luck on their side, and because of the prior lifestyle Karen led before her tragic end, the police were able to match the teeth of the deceased to those of Karen Olson Anderson. They never learned who had made the call.

All anyone knew of her was that she lived by herself. Some knew she had two children. That bit of information remained out of the police report. Those who cared for her children assumed her two children had gotten away. When no other bodies were found in the wreckage, no one mentioned the children.

With no other questions asked or follow-up done, the police designated the case closed. Another drunken fool had died. No one wanted anyone to know that anyone in the vicinity knew her. The only good that came out of the mess was for her children.

No one remembered, or missed, the old jalopy.

Chapter 6

Unable to sleep in the cold car, Ralph awoke cold and stiff. Sitting up, he found Vanessa already awake, curled into a corner, shivering.

"Damn," Ralph grunted, "Why didn't you wake me?"

Getting into the front seat, Ralph quickly got the car started and turned on the heater.

"I wish I knew what time it is," Ralph said.

"I'm cold and hungry," Vanessa told him.

Having filled the gas tank last night, before pulling behind the station for sleep, Ralph drove away. Still cold, even with the heater going, Vanessa cuddled her brother's side. Eventually, they began to feel warm again. Twice, Ralph had to pull over and close his eyes. The last time was to eat and get gas. Each time he stopped, Vanessa would awaken.

"While I'm getting gas, go into the cafe and get something to eat," he told her. "When I'm done, I'll join you."

Joining his sister, they ate burgers and drank coffee. As they ate, they began to feel the warmth flowing through them. Ralph remembered the many times during the night, as he drove onward, the lights from the oncoming cars blinded him. What little he had driven as a kid was never at night.

Now with something in his belly, he knew he needed sleep. Even with the fear someone was chasing them, Ralph knew they had to stop before they had an accident. Warm, they nestled down in the car for some sleep. When they awoke, they felt somewhat rested, better than he did the night before.

Behind the wheel, Ralph drove on. Every now and then, he would gaze at his sister. She was curled up in the seat next to him, sleeping. He still could not believe they were doing this. Vanessa did seem comfortable, not in the least afraid. It was the only time Vanessa seemed her age, as far as Ralph could remember.

When they had crossed the State line, Ralph knew he either had to change cars or get the old Chevy painted. He did feel somewhat safe because of the disguises they wore. In the quiet of the night, with Vanessa sleeping next to him, Ralph drove on.

Right after they left home, Ralph drove to Harvey's garage hoping to get a quick, cheap paint job. Harvey had been a great guy to let him rebuild the car in his garage. Harvey's garage sat on the outskirts of town. Old wrecked junks and cars needing repairs lined the property. It was from the junk cars Ralph got his parts for the old Chevrolet. With Harvey's help, Ralph learned how to fix cars.

Harvey, a tall, skinny young man near thirty, knew of Ralph's problem. He was willing to help Ralph in any way he could, as long as he remained out of trouble with the law. Harvey was always in dirty, greasy T-shirts and coveralls. His face and hands were stained with the color of the grease.

Besides always needing a shave and a haircut, Harvey looked as if he never bathed. However, to Ralph, Harvey was the most trusted friend anyone could have. Harvey would do anything for a friend.

Knowing Ralph's problem, it scared Harvey to think his friend could do that sort of damage to one of his mom's men.

"You didn't kill him, did you?" Harvey asked.

"I think maybe I did, I don't know for sure," Ralph mumbled.

"Well then, the sooner you get away from here, the better off you will be," Harvey told him.

"What if the police spotted this car?" Ralph had asked.

"Only if they know what they are looking for."

"Don't you think my mom will tell them?"

"Shit, she's always too drunk to pay attention."

"I hope you're right," Ralph said.

"We have to take that chance. Now get the hell out of here."

With disguises, Ralph was transformed into looking older. He went to see his sister. Seeing the finished product amazed Ralph. Her beauty held his attention. Having helped Vanessa with part of her transformation, Ralph thought he would have a good idea what she would look like. He was completely wrong. She looked to be in her late teens.

Being it was the first time Vanessa had ever worn high heels, she had trouble walking in them. She knew she would have to get used to the change. Their getaway depended on it. Unknown to Vanessa, Harvey had slipped four hundred dollars to Ralph.

"Pay me when you get the money," Harvey told him quietly, "and good luck."

The four hundred Harvey gave him, added to the eighty dollars he already had, Ralph felt they now had enough money to make their escape.

"Thanks, Harvey, I won't forget this."

"If you ever find a place to settle and you like it, well, maybe I'll move there too."

"I'd like that," Ralph told him, as they shook hands.

Once they left the garage, Ralph knew they were finally on their own. There will be no turning back now.

It was just getting to be daylight when the lights of a truck stop appeared.

"Vanessa," he called, shaking her.

"We are stopping for food and gas. While we are in a restaurant or when we are around other people, you will have to act like we're newlyweds." Ralph told her.

"You mean cuddle and kiss and all that stuff?" she said, giggling.

"Yeah," he sighed, "But not too much. After all, you are my sister."

"I know," she sighed, "But we do sleep together like a married couple, don't we?"

"We sleep together, yes, but not like a married couple."

"What do they do differently?" she asked.

"They do what mom does, only with love instead of for money."

"I understand that, but don't newlyweds cuddle and kiss all the time?" she asked, trying to be serious.

"You know they do, but try to keep it to a minimum," he said, "Remember, we are brother and sister."

"Don't worry, I won't overact, but we do have to make people believe us, don't we?" **she excitedly said.**

Turning away from her brother, Vanessa concealed the devil and mischief that lit her eyes. Feeling he was being played by his sister, Ralph became worried. With only four hundred eighty dollars between them, Ralph knew he would have to find a job and soon. They had already spent thirty dollars for gas, plus another ten on food, leaving them with four hundred forty dollars.

Chapter 7

After filling their bellies and feeding the car, they drove away. Exhausted, but wanting to get as far away as possible, Ralph drove a few extra hours on deserted back roads. It was getting late on the third day, and they had been traveling a long time and needed rest. Around the next corner, a sign caught Ralph's eye. Deciding to stop for a rest and get something to eat, Ralph slowed to a crawl so he wouldn't miss the turn.

Pulling in, the first thing Ralph noticed was the small sandwich shop sitting quite a distance from the road. Ralph liked the privacy it afforded. At the motel, Ralph got a room. After putting their things in their room, they walked to the café. Entering the small café, through the back door, Ralph led his sister to a booth close to the back door.

Seated, they studied the menu while waiting for the waitress to come to the table. Ralph wanted to stay away from the windows. Gazing around the room, he found the room small but cozy. Only a hand full of truckers occupied the counter space.

All the booths were empty except the one they were using. As Ralph nervously turned his attention back to the menu, neither he nor Vanessa saw or heard the server come to the table.

"What can I do for the two of you?" the waitress asked, in a deep raspy voice.

"Burgers and fries please," Ralph replied.

"Anything to drink?" she asked.

"What do you want, honey?" Ralph asked Vanessa.

So far, their little ploy seemed to be working.

"The same as you, my sweetheart," Vanessa said, with a low sexy voice.

Watching his sister as she spoke, Ralph couldn't help but see the loving look in her eyes.

Turning to the server, Ralph said, "Two chocolate shakes."

"Thank you."

Ralph watched the server walk away. She was an older woman, with gray hair and a round body. All the extra weight the waitress was carrying made her body jiggle as she walked. All the servers were wearing the same old clothing, a black dress and white apron. Seeing the waitress looking so tired and sore when she walked, Ralph began to feel sorry for her.

Beginning to relax, Ralph turned to his sister. He realized that while he was talking to the server, Vanessa surprised him by moving closer to him. He didn't notice her movement until she placed her hand on his thigh. Now, so as not to cause any suspicion, he put his arm over her shoulders. In response, she melted against him. Not wanting to make a scene, he hugged her close.

Bending to kiss her on the cheek, Ralph got a surprise when Vanessa, anticipating the move, took advantage of the situation by meeting his kiss with a kiss of her own. It was a small kiss, but a kiss on the lips nevertheless. Once the waitress was gone, Ralph turned to face her.

"You're doing a great job selling your older age," Ralph told her.

"This is fun acting older," she giggled, "I like making believe we are married."

"I have to admit, you do look a lot older dressed the way you are."

"Yeah, and I have tits too."

Excited, Vanessa placed her hands on her breasts.

"Hey, watch it," Ralph said, "People might see you doing that."

Quickly dropping her hands to her lap, embarrassed, Vanessa's face turned bright red. Laughing at the situation, Ralph had to look away. Vanessa poked him in the ribs.

"Don't laugh at me. I didn't think about that."

"I'm not laughing at you, just your reaction."

"I won't do that again," she grinned.

Quickly, his smile disappeared. Thoughts of later, when they had to stop for the night, suddenly made him feel nervous. Then he saw in his mind a real bed, where they could get some needed rest. Worrying about the disguises, he hoped they would hold up at a motel. Ralph's reverie was broken when the server bringing the food set it on the table before them.

"Could I get you anything else?" the server asked.

"No, thank you," Vanessa told her.

Acting nonchalantly, Ralph watched his sister eat. Amazingly, she acted as an adult at times. Feeling more secure, with each passing moment, about their situation, Ralph began to relax more.

As they ate, Ralph suddenly, with no reason, became nervous. He had a feeling, something he couldn't explain, was going to happen. He felt they didn't have much time to waste.

As soon as they finished their food, Ralph paid the cashier. Another ten dollars was gone, he realized. Off the top of his head, he tried to think of how much they had left. They had four hundred and thirty dollars left, and they had to stop for the night.

Ralph refused to let Vanessa freeze another night in the car. Even though they still had over four hundred dollars, Ralph knew it wouldn't be too long before they ran out of money.

"We don't have much money left, Vanessa. I'm going to have to get a job somewhere and soon."

"Do you have some place in mind?"

"No, but along this coast would be great."

"I'd like that too," she said, "Any place as long as I'm with you."

Pulling out of the parking lot, they drove a few more miles before they hit the freeway. Taking the freeway, it wouldn't be long before they reached the coastline, heading north toward Washington. Having never seen the ocean before, Ralph slowed the car each time to get a glimpse of the awesome beauty around them.

"Look at that," Ralph said excitedly, "that's awesome, isn't it?"

"Can we stop?" Vanessa said, reverting back to her young age for a moment.

Liking what he saw and to please his sister, Ralph turned off at the next pullout and stopped. The sight, from where they stopped, was beautiful. Sitting near the edge of a high cliff, overlooking the ocean, they watched huge waves break over huge jagged protruding rocks. For an instant, the waves would cover the rocks, then as if by magic, the rocks would reappear.

Both he and Vanessa were enthralled with what looked like a white foamy substance that covered the rocks each time the waves broke over them. As soon as the water receded, the rocks would reappear; another wave would roll in, covering the rocks again. Repeatedly, as if by clockwork, the waves rolled in then out, never changing, never deviating, unless a larger or smaller wave rolled in.

"We had better get going, Vanessa. We don't want to get stuck in this car again tonight, do we?"

"No, I agree," she said sadly, "But maybe we can stop for the night near a beach."

"I'll try and find a place like that," he told her. "It would be fun to walk in the sand."

Leaning over, Vanessa kissed her brother on the cheek.

"I love you, Ralph."

Turning to her, without thinking about it, he kissed her quickly on the lips. Realizing what he had just done, he put the car in gear. So, he would keep his attention on the road. He took a deep breath. With a sigh, Ralph pulled out onto the highway once more.

Traveling on, a few more miles up the road, they came to another opening in the trees. Again, the ocean came into view. This time instead of huge craggy rocks, there was a large span of a sandy beach. Smaller waves rolled back and forth on the sandy beach.

"Would you like to walk on the beach?" Ralph asked his sister.

"Sure. I would love to, but do we have the time?" she asked.

"We'll make time," Ralph told her.

Pulling completely off the road, he parked. Getting out of the car, they walked a few feet until they came to a path leading down the embankment. Reaching the bottom, they walked through the sand to the water edge. Standing closer to the edge than they should, a small wave caught them at the ankles, filling their shoes with wet sand. With shoes full of sand, their feet became heavy and uncomfortable with each step.

"I think we had better take our shoes off from now on," Ralph said.

"We should do that now and give them a chance to dry," Vanessa told him.

"You're a smart girl. What would I do without you?"

"Nothing, I hope. I need you in my life too."

Sitting in the sand, they removed their wet shoes and socks. After cleaning the sludge from their shoes, they carried them with them, as they wandered down the beach. Barefoot, the feeling of the warm sand sifting between their toes felt like nothing they had ever felt before. Every few moments, they stopped to pick seashells and kelp from the sand.

Excited at never having seen objects such as these, they forgot about how much time had passed. They were having too much fun to think of anything else. All of a sudden, time seemed to pass quickly for them. Looking at his watch, Ralph realized it was getting late.

"Maybe it would better to move on and find a place to sleep for the night. It will be getting dark soon."

"Do we have too? I am having so much fun. I haven't had this much fun in years."

"Me either, but we need to get going."

"All right," she said, reverting back to her actual age.

Without wearing their shoes and socks, they felt every small rock on the path dig into their bare feet. Finally reaching the road, Ralph helped his sister up. Hand in hand they walked the fifteen feet to the car.

Along the way, they passed many small beaches. Ralph longed to stop again, to breathe the cool fresh air, while the brisk wind rushed through his hair. He also wanted to feel again what the sand felt like between his toes. However, it was getting late, and they had to find a place for the night. Ralph was beginning to get concerned a few hours later. Nightfall was setting upon them.

Chapter 8

With the sun setting, every time they were able to see the ocean, the water seemed to turn into different colors. Those reflections off the water were one of the images that helped keep him awake.

Rounding the next corner, Ralph saw a neon sign, over the trees, to a small motel just off the road to their right. Remembering he had passed through the main part of town a couple of miles back, he felt safe staying this far out of town. He pulled his old Chevy into the driveway next to the sign saying Office.

Parking, he slumped in his seat. He needed to close his eyes for just a few moments to relax. While resting his eyes, Ralph tried clearing his mind to think. Even though his heart and pulse were racing wildly, he knew he had better compose himself before going into the motel office to get a room. He didn't need to raise suspicion or to make a mistake. He and his sister had a part to play.

"Now don't forget, if I need you inside, play it cool," he told her.

"I won't forget, I promise."

Weary, Ralph slowly got out of the car. It felt so good to be standing on solid ground again. He had begun to feel cramped behind the wheel of his car. Taking a few moments to stretch, he surveyed his surroundings. The Motel was single-floor and small. From what he could see, it had maybe twenty rooms, the most, if that many.

In seconds, a brisk breeze picked up, making him shiver. Then, as fast as the breeze came, it disappeared, making the air warmer. In the background, he could hear what sounded like waves breaking on the beach. From the sound, they had to be close to the beach to hear the surf.

Hoping to see the beach, Ralph stared intently into the darkness in the direction the sound was coming. Even with the moon full overhead, he couldn't see what he was looking for. As Ralph turned back toward the car, his eye caught sight of a sign in front of the motel.

"Jake's Restaurant"

Immediately, a smile crossed his face. It was nice. A small restaurant seemed to be attached to the front of the motel. As hungry as they were, it was funny neither of them noticed the sign when he pulled into the motel.

First, he thought he had to register for a room. After getting their room and settled in, they could go to the café for something to eat. Standing outside trying to clear his head, Ralph knew what he wanted to say. He had rehearsed it a dozen times or more. Now ready to face their first test, he took a deep breath.

Climbing three steps, leading to the office, Ralph first glanced back at Vanessa, just for just an instant. Then opening the door, he stepped inside. The room was warm and cozy, smelling of apple cinnamon. The sudden warmth that was surrounding Ralph made him realize how chilly the outside air was getting.

Standing at the counter, Ralph noticed the small brass bell lying on the counter. Quickly hitting the button on top, he waited for the attendant to appear. When the attendant didn't quickly appear, Ralph began scanning the room.

Along one wall were two brown chairs, a brown couch, and a small desk with literature upon it. On the counter, next to the bell, a rack of maps and pamphlets with useful information.

Finally, an older man with silver hair and a scraggily beard to match came in from an adjoining room. Wearing a red and yellow plaid shirt and baggy khaki pants, he limped in with the aid of a cane. Immediately, Ralph's mouth became dry. Frightened, he suddenly found it difficult to speak.

"Do you have any rooms?"

Ralph's lack of confidence made the old man weary.

"You're in luck," he said, "We have one room left."

The old man eyed Ralph so closely, Ralph began to feel nervous.

"How much is a room?" Ralph asked.

"It'll cost you thirty a night."

As the old man spoke, he moved toward the window. At the window, the old man bent slightly as he peered out the window. Ralph knew the old man was trying to see who was in the car. Now was not the time to be coy.

"My wife and I are on our honeymoon," Ralph uttered. "Could you come down a few dollars for just one night?"

Starting to feel more confident again, Ralph's manner started to change.

"Where is the wife?" The old man asked, in a raspy voice. All of a sudden, the old man started coughing.

"In the car," Ralph said, a little flustered.

Ralph had not expected the man to ask that question. The old man, used to meeting different lifestyles, noticed Ralph's uneasiness right away.

"You look a little too young to be married, young man. Do you have a marriage license?"

"Yes, I do."

Reaching into his pants, Ralph pulled out his wallet. Producing the fake license, he handed it to the old man. Then moving to the door, Ralph called Vanessa inside.

"Vanessa, honey, could you come in here for a moment?"

Entering the office, Vanessa acted tired, moving slowly. Stopping at the counter, Vanessa moved against her brother, slipping her arm through his arm. Looking at her brother, with the most loving stare she could muster, she smiled up at him.

"Is there any trouble, honey?"

After seeing Vanessa and the license, the old man seemed satisfied; they were a legal couple.

"No trouble, ma'am," the old man coughed, "I just needed to see you and the license."

"You did give him the license, didn't you?" Vanessa asked.

"I've got it all here, no problem." The old man said, handing the license back to Ralph.

"Good," she said, hugging Ralph's arm to her breast.

"Here are the keys to your room, number ten. The room is at the end of the building."

Taking the key, Ralph thanked him, then led his sister to the door smiling.

"One can't be too careful now days you know," they heard the old man say, as they closed the door. It was the first time the old man had smiled, while doing business.

Outside, Ralph let out a sigh of relief. They had passed the first hurdle.

CHAPTER 9

The room was light blue in color and dinky, but clean. On one wall was the air-conditioner. On another wall, a small color television, chained to a stand anchored to the wall. Showing so much distrust by the owners, who must have lost a few televisions in the past.

No sooner had they entered the room than Vanessa flopped on the bed. Bouncing a few times, she began to giggle. Ralph was happy this trip didn't take the bounce away from his sister. Let her act like a child. She needed this outlet at the moment. She was far too young to be acting like an adult for the rest of her life.

"This feels so good," she said, stretching.

As she continued to bounce, the springs squeaked. Ralph wasn't sure how long the bed could take such punishment.

"We'll have to do this later tonight, so people will think we are having sex," she said.

Ignoring his sister, Ralph said, "It looks like we're going to have to sleep together tonight. This happens to be the only bed in the room."

"That's all right with me," she said cheerfully, "I like you next to me at night anyway. You make me feel comfortable."

"Are you hungry?" Ralph asked, changing the subject.

"I'm starving."

"We don't have much money, so go easy."

After spending thirty dollars for the room, they were now down to four hundred even. They had to eat breakfast and get gas. That should be another thirty dollars.

"What will we do when we don't have any money?" Vanessa asked.

"I hope to get a job before that."

"What if you don't?"

"I'll cross that bridge when I get to it."

That seemed to satisfy her, for the moment.

"Let's go to the beach, after we eat," Ralph said, feeling youthful and not quite as tired as he was when they got here. He was ready to explore.

"But it's dark outside," Vanessa said, grabbing her brother's hand and sighing. With her hand feeling good in his, for some assurance, Ralph gave her hand a little squeeze.

"Afraid of the dark," he teased.

"What are we waiting for?" Vanessa said, jumping up.

Quickly moving toward the door, she had to hesitate, knowing her brother had not moved.

"We have to eat first," Ralph told her.

Locking the door behind them, Ralph put the key in his pocket. Then, walking slowly across the gravel parking lot, holding his sister's hand, they got to the restaurant. As he tried to release her hand, she stubbornly gripped his hand tighter.

Ralph realized she didn't want to let his hand go. Opening the door to the restaurant, Ralph let her take the first step inside. Inside, the restaurant seemed smaller inside than from the outside.

Following his sister inside, a sweet smell of food cooking filled the air, intensifying his hunger. Glancing around, he noticed twelve tables covered with blue and white checkered tablecloths. Each table had, beside the condiments, a small plastic vase with ornamental flowers in it.

The room felt homey, clean, warm, and comfortable.

Seeing the only table available was next to a window, crossing the room, they gladly took the seat. Immediately, a young blond boy server, not much older than Ralph, came to the table. Even though they were starving, they ordered light, trying to conserve what money they had left.

"How far is the beach from here?" Vanessa asked the boy before he could get away.

"Maybe two or three hundred yards," he told her. "There is a path just across the road, leading through the brush."

Ralph became nervous, the way the young waiter kept staring at his sister. He seemed to be enthralled with her beauty.

"We can hear the waves, but we couldn't see them," Ralph said, trying to change the boy's thought patterns.

"That's because of the trees and bushes. To get there at night, you will need a flashlight," he said.

Turning his attention, again, to the business at hand, Vanessa had helped the situation by showing the rings she wore.

"Thanks," Vanessa said, flirting with him.

After the boy left with their order, Ralph vented his jealousy.

"Why did you have to openly flirt with him?" Ralph asked in a whisper.

"If I didn't know better, I would say you are jealous."

"Not at all," Ralph lied, "you just need to be a little more secretive."

"I'm sorry," Vanessa said in her hurt voice. "I've never had the chance to flirt before. The thought of it seemed like it would be fun."

"I know, and I want you to have fun, but we also have to be careful."

"Are we still going to the beach after we eat?" Vanessa asked, trying to change the subject.

"I said we would, didn't I?" he snarled.

My brother is jealous and still angry, she thought, hoping he would get over his jealousy.

By the time the food came, they were famished. The food tasted as good as it smelled. There was enough food to fill them.

Finished, Ralph decided to show his authority. Getting up from the table, he helped his sister up. Then, keeping her hand in his, they crossed the room to the register. The young man was watching. After paying, Ralph took his sister's hand and led her from the diner. Ralph made sure their fingers were laced, like lovers.

Standing just outside the door of the restaurant, Vanessa made her move. Before Ralph knew what was happening, Vanessa wanted to make it clear she was his wife, to anyone watching.

Placing her arms around her brother's neck, she pulled his face down to hers for a loving kiss. She knew her brother wouldn't pull away. He was much too conscious of making a good show.

As Vanessa expected, Ralph didn't pull away. He definitely didn't want to make a scene. To make the show better, Ralph wrapped his arms around Vanessa's waist and pulled her tightly to him. Returning her kiss with more fervor than he intended, he felt her lips soften under his.

Just for an instant, he liked the feel of her sweet kiss and her body, even if it was with all its faults padding. In his mind, Vanessa didn't feel so young. Her lips and padded body pressing against his had an effect on him he didn't like much.

"I love you, Ralph," she said.

Their arms remained wrapped around each other, even after stopping the kiss.

"I love you, too, Vanessa."

For added punctuation, he gave his sister another shorter kiss, then let her go. Reluctantly, she let him go, but held on to him all the way back to the room.

Chapter 10

Quickly gathering a flashlight from his bag. Not knowing what else they would need, Ralph took two towels from the rack in the bathroom. Armed with what he thought they needed for the walk to the beach, he quickly went back into the bedroom to get his sister.

"If you still want to go to the beach, let's go," he said.

"Do you have a flashlight, like the boy said?" she asked.

Showing her the flashlight and the towels, he smiled. As they left the room, a blast of cool air blew over them. Like youngsters, instead of putting on something warm, they put their arms around each other as they walked.

Following the directions the boy gave them, they made their way down the dark, winding path. Without the flashlight, someone would have gotten hurt. Without the flashlight, the trek would have been too difficult. Not only was the path filled with small loose stones and visible roots projecting through the ground, but branches with sharp thorns also lined the path. In the dark, they would have stumbled or slipped on the many hazards, maybe even getting injured.

The beach wasn't as far from the motel as they feared it would be. In the daylight, they would be able to see the beach clearly through the trees and bushes. With the moon high and full, its light reflected off the water.

After reaching the soft sand, they looked in both directions to see if they were alone on the beach. Not far from where they stood, huge, partially burnt logs lay scattered on the sand. Some were partially buried in the sand. One of the logs not too far away afforded them a good place to sit.

Shedding their shoes and socks, they placed them with the flashlight and towels next to the log. Like two small children, they strolled hand in hand to the water's edge. The sand, where they had taken off their shoes, felt great between his toes. The surface was still a little warm from the day's sun.

When they reached the edge of the water, they stuck their feet into the waves. As the cold water washed over their feet and ankles, they were shocked. Letting out a scream, Vanessa ran back to the warmer sand. Laughing, Ralph stayed where he was, letting the cold water lap his feet.

"Come on, chicken. Once you get used to it, it isn't so cold."

Not wanting to be outdone, Vanessa went back to where her brother was standing. Ralph couldn't help but laugh at the expression on Vanessa's face as her feet came in contact with the cold water once again.

Needing and wanting to feel the cold water on his tired and sore feet, Ralph rolled up the legs of his trousers above his knees. Seeing what her brother was doing, Vanessa picked her dress up to the waist. Holding her dress with one hand, Ralph was able to see the padded underclothing she was wearing.

"Vanessa, why don't you take that stuff off for the night? It will cool you down and you would be able to have more fun."

"What if someone comes?"

"Who will know the difference? Besides, you don't want to get them wet."

"Where will I go?"

"Back up in the trees. I'll go with you, just in case you need help."

In the trees, Vanessa rid herself of her padding by stripping down naked. The sight of her small nude body was a sight Ralph would never forget. Putting her outer clothing back on, Vanessa found the clothes loose on her slender body. Placing the padding with their shoes and socks, Vanessa took Ralph's hand and race with him back to the water.

Wading out to their knees, they enjoyed the feel of the small waves lapping against the rolled-up clothing. Standing close together, they embraced the other's waist for support. Standing, they basked in the coolness of the night. It took a while before their bodies adjusted to the cold water.

Out of the cold, dark depths, a larger wave rolled in, catching them above the knees. As the frigid water washed over their private parts, they had trouble catching their breaths. Unexpectedly, another huge wave, larger than the last, rolled in, catching them high above the waist.

Turning back toward shore, they were not quick enough. Another wave caught them from behind, knocking them to their knees. Landing face first in the water, they came up sputtering and coughing. As they came up, for a breath of air, Ralph could feel the undertow as it threatened to pull them out to sea.

Digging his hands and feet into the sand to stop his slide, Ralph felt the force lessening against him. Getting to his feet, Ralph heard the scream of a frightened Vanessa.

With the force of the water lessened, Ralph had time to help his sister. On his feet, he pulled her up and steadied her. As he pushed her forward, toward the safety of the beach, another wave swamped him. This time the undertow took him. As the water receded, it began dragging him out to sea. Vanessa was able to crawl to safety.

Suddenly, like an act of God, a huge wave swooped in, catching Ralph above the waist. The momentum of the wave cast him higher upon the beach. This time as the water receded, the drag on him lessened. Almost out of breath, Ralph managed to get to his hands and knees. Using his last ounce of strength, he tried crawling out of reach of the waves.

He hadn't gotten far enough away. The next wave knocked his knees from beneath him. Seeing her brother's peril, Vanessa grasped her brother's wrists, while digging her feet into the sand. It took all her strength to hold him back from the sea.

A lull in the waves gave Vanessa the time she needed to drag her brother farther into the drier sand, far enough to be out of harm's way.

Now on dry sand, too exhausted to move, they lay huddled together as they tried to keep warm and catch their breath. With bodies dripping with sand and water, they began to shiver from the cold. While the waves were tossing them about in the surf, the wind seemed warm. Now soaked to the skin, the wind chilled their bones.

After a few minutes, when the cold started to overtake them, they used their last ounce of strength to get to their feet. Kneeling next to each other, they used the other for support.

Finally getting to their feet, they staggered back to the log where their clothing lay. Freezing, they retrieved their valuables. Wrapping up in the towels, to help keep them warm, they staggered sluggishly back to their room.

Once they were safe and back in their room, the combination of fear and cold night air they had experienced made Vanessa begin to violently shake. Unable to control her shaking, Ralph peeled his sister's clothes from her tiny body.

With no thought of modesty, Ralph shed his own clothing to rid his body of wet clothing. Not thinking of his own nudity, Ralph grabbed one of the towels lying on the bed and began drying his sister briskly. Only when his hand moved over his sister's small breasts did Ralph realize his kid sister was beginning to sprout. The feel of her small breast in his hand shocked him.

Quickly pulling his hand away, he gazed down her naked body. At twelve, she was already getting hair in her pubic area. It was then, he realized Vanessa was looking at him too. She had seen her brother naked before, but never this close.

Still needing more warmth, Ralph made a quick decision. His need to get his sister warm made Ralph make one of two choices. Take her either to bed and use his body to warm her or to get her into a hot shower. She was shaking so violently he would have to hold her steady until she was somewhat back to her normal state.

Not wanting his sister to catch a cold, Ralph quickly made the decision. Pulling her with him, Ralph got her into the hot shower. Standing in the hot shower, holding his sister's shaking body steady, even he felt the relief of the hot water, as it careened over their frozen bodies. With the hot water careening down their bodies, Vanessa clung to her brother for added support.

Remaining in the shower longer than usual, both felt exhaustion hit them. With their bodies thawed, they stepped apart. Feeling half normal again, they stepped from the shower. They dried themselves briskly, until they could feel their circulation returning.

Vanessa was the first to run to the bedroom. Too tired to find and put on her night gown, she slipped into bed naked. Liking the feel of the sheets against her naked skin, Vanessa wrapped the blankets tightly around her.

When Ralph came out of the bathroom a few minutes later, Vanessa couldn't help but notice his penis, the way it swung so freely between his huge, solid thighs. All of a sudden, she was more alert about their surroundings.

"Hurry to bed, darling," Vanessa teased.

Turning to face her, he saw she was holding the covers open for him to join her. Before going to bed, he walked across the room to open the window. As the cool fresh air swooped in, an involuntary shiver shook his body.

As quickly as he could, not thinking of anything but staying warm, Ralph slid beneath the covers. As he joined his sister in bed, he got a view of his sister's young, youthful nude body. Still not thinking clearly, as he crawled in next to her, he tried not letting what he saw faze him.

Both were naked and neither had ever slept in the nude before. Under the covers, another shiver shook him, making him want to get warm again. Now in the warm bed, he felt the warmth of his sister lying close to him.

"Move closer, honey," she crooned, "I need your warm body next to mine for warmth."

Needing her warmth and comfort, he slid closer to her. As he wound his arms around her shoulders, she snuggled close for warmth. Suddenly, a feeling of special kinship surged through them. Lying stiff and naked, pressed against each other, Ralph began to realize her nudity was going to pose a problem.

Lying naked next to him, in the same bed naked, was also strange to Vanessa. Never in all the years they shared a bed had they ever slept naked.

"I like the feel of your strong body holding me," she whispered.

The room was quickly getting colder, but the bed was warm. Ralph allowed his sister to stay in his arms. They had slept like this all their lives, he thought, just not naked.

Feeling warmer, Ralph tried rolling away from her. Vanessa didn't allow that. Comfortable, warm, and now drowsy, Vanessa laid her head on her brother's shoulder. As she cuddled him, she placed her free arm around his waist, leaving the other pinned between their bodies.

Trying to relax, Ralph found his mind working against him. Thoughts, he shouldn't be having bombarded him. As Vanessa snuggled closer to him, his feelings deepened. Unable to get comfortable, Ralph was acutely aware of her small, bare breasts pressing against his side.

Extreme uncomfortable feelings surged through his body. He was about to have her move to her side when she threw a leg over his body. Immediately, his imagination ran wild. Taking a deep breath, he held it. Damn, I shouldn't be thinking of these things. He relaxed a bit when he heard her softly breathing, knowing she was asleep.

Chapter 11

Morning came too soon for Ralph and Vanessa. Still feeling a little exhausted from last night's scare and knowing their bodies needed more rest, Ralph contemplated staying another day. Then, thinking about the money they had left, he changed his mind.

Three hundred and seventy dollars was all they had left, and with no money coming in, he had to conserve. Glancing at his sister, curled up on her side of the bed, still sound asleep, he felt sorry for her.

She must have rolled away sometime during the night. She had to be very exhausted, too. However, they probably had a lot of ground to cover, and they didn't have that much money to spend. Making his decision, he rolled from the bed.

Deciding to get up and have an early start, Ralph let Vanessa sleep while he showered. After a quick shower, he dressed, then picked up the room. He wanted to be sure nothing would be left behind. Not until he was sure they had everything and everything packed, did he wake her.

"Vanessa, wake up. It's time to get up and take your shower," Ralph said softly. "Before we get underway, we'll go to the café for something to eat."

Rolling over, Vanessa gazed sleepily into her brother's eyes. Not wanting to argue, she slipped out of bed, naked and unashamed. He couldn't help but watch his sister as she moved toward the bathroom. Images of her young, petite body flashed in front of his face.

Seeing the small rise of her breasts and the sparse hair between her thighs made him think. Now, her hip movement as she moved, for a twelve-year-old, was astounding. In another year or so, she will be gorgeous. Just watching Vanessa move made Ralph grow with need. Needing not to have those thoughts, while she showered, he packed the car.

It was only eight in the morning when they stepped from their room to have breakfast. A thick, dense fog covered the land. The air seemed thick and damp with small drops of dew wetting their clothes. They could feel the cold as they walked.

Upon reaching the small café, when they entered, Ralph was happy they had a different waiter. This time it was a cute young girl. As they ate their small breakfast, Ralph nearly changed his mind about staying at the motel for another day or two.

Making up his mind would be easy, but he knew they had little choice. Trying to conserve their money, as much as they wanted to stay, he knew they had to move on.

On the road, time passed quickly. Driving up the coast, they saw more of the ocean and beaches, but couldn't afford to stop. Hours later, after stopping in a few towns looking for work, Ralph was getting discouraged. Unable to find any kind of work or suitable living quarters, and having to still buy food and gas, was turning into a hardship.

After passing through several small coastal towns without finding work, Ralph made his final decision. Because all the towns they passed through were small, as much as they would love to live at the coast, Ralph knew they would have to go inward, to larger cities for work.

It was sad that all the towns they passed through, on their way up the coast, were the same. Along the main drags had gas stations, banks, coffee shops, and grocery-hardware stores combined.

This town seemed a little different. It wasn't much bigger than the other towns, but it did have more to it. Though the main drag was the same, off the main drag, they could see a church steeple above the trees and a few houses scattered in the hills.

This particular town ended at a large river. The river divided one town from another. Ralph thought about driving over the huge green rotating bridge to the town on the other side. Sitting at the edge of the road, he thought about it, but then, realizing all towns along the coast were all the same as the next, he decided against it.

"I think our best chance is to head inland to find what we're looking for. We've wasted enough time in these dinky towns along the coast," Ralph sighed. "Maybe the opportunities will be better inland."

"I don't care where we go as long as I'm with you. Any place will be fine," she said, touching his shoulder for support.

Taking the other road, that looked like a main highway, he began following the river. As they began following the river, a sprinkling of homes could be seen stuck away in the hills. Other homes, he was sure, had to be nestled somewhere between the hills behind the main drag.

The further he drove he was sure he had made the right decision. Followed the road along the winding river. The view was beautiful. It wasn't long before Ralph started doubting himself. As they left the town behind, the river road didn't seem to be heading anywhere. Had he made a mistake? Unknown to Ralph at the moment, before the day ended, his decision would be well-founded.

Following the river, Vanessa moved away from her spot by the door. Moving close to her brother, she hugged his arm while laying her head on his shoulder.

She trusted him with my life, she thought to herself, and she loved him more than life itself. She didn't know what she would do without him.

The drive was so beautiful. Ralph drove slowly upriver. Gazing at the few homes sitting at the river's edge, he couldn't help thinking. "Wouldn't it be neat to have a house along a river like this?" Ralph murmured.

"Yeah, we could have a boat and go fishing," Vanessa said.

Some were small farms or shacks, while others were nice homes. One home in particular stood out from the others. It had to have a grand view from where it sat on the hill overlooking the river.

"I wonder what it would be like to live in a place like that?" he said, pointing to the huge house on the hill.

"How would you like to live in a place like that?" He asked her.

"It would be great, but when you get married, we won't be able to live together."

"Why not?"

"Because I will get jealous if you with the other woman."

Soon, they were away from the town. Ralph hoped to find a place to live and work soon. He did not want to be stranded, out here in the middle of nowhere. The last time he looked, they had only two hundred and sixty dollars left.

About five miles inland, they entered a canyon. The walls of the canyon rose one hundred feet or more above them. The road wound through the canyon hugging the river. For twenty miles, Ralph followed the winding road and river. All the sights were awesome and very beautiful. A few small islands were scattered along the twenty-mile stretch. One of the bigger islands caught his eye.

I'm going to come back to that island and search it out one day, he thought. All was quiet in the canyon, except for the sounds of the tires singing on the asphalt, and the thundering sound of the rushing river as it careened over projecting and sunken boulders. During the twenty-mile trek, only two other vehicles were seen going the opposite direction.

It would soon be getting dark. By the time they emerged from the canyon onto a large city road, there were only three or so hours left of daylight. When they finally emerged from the canyon, onto another main drag, signs indicated there were towns in both directions.

Wanting to go north, to get as far away from their past life as possible, Ralph headed in the northerly direction. Taking the northern route, they had to make a slight climb for close to a mile to the top. At the top, Ralph pulled into a truck pullout and stopped. Not far from the top of the grade, Ralph knew he had found what they had been looking for. Not quite dark yet, Ralph was still able to see quite clearly.

The town itself was nestled in a forest of pine at the edge of a large lake. The lake seemed to be the origin of the river that flowed through the canyon to the ocean.

Almost out of money, Ralph knew this had to be the town they would settle in. Actually, they didn't have much choice; their money was running out. After the night at the motel, gas, and food, they had less than one hundred dollars left. They couldn't get much further on what little money they had.

Chapter 12

After descending the hill, Ralph began driving slowly through the town. Looking for that special place, he would know it when he saw it. Almost through town, Ralph began to feel depressed again. There didn't seem to be anything in this town either. Stopping at the last red light in town, he waited for the light to turn green.

Suddenly, without warning or reason, Ralph turned right. As he began driving out of town, on this back road that probably led nowhere, he was beginning to think what he did was kind of dumb, but something on the back of his mind told him to try it. He didn't hear words. He just had a feeling.

Luck was with him. He hadn't driven very far, just a short way out of town, when something caught his attention. Out of the corner of his eye, Ralph caught a glimpse of some run-down cabins almost hidden behind the trees. They actually sat behind an old gas station. Almost out of gas, Ralph decided to stop, get gas, and ask about the cabins.

Pulling into the station, he didn't have to blow his horn. A grizzly old man with a gray scraggly beard and wearing a dirty plaid shirt with torn Levi's came out to wait on them. Not only did he look old, he smelled older. He probably hadn't had a shower or bath for most of his life. He was a huge man with spindly legs and a huge potbelly. His smile showed he had a few missing teeth. What teeth he did have in his mouth were rotten.

"Are those cabins for rent?" Ralph asked.

"They would be, Sonny, if I could ever get them fixed."

Ralph had to pull his head back from the smell. An unbearable odor came from the man's mouth, making him nauseous.

"What's wrong with them?" Ralph asked.

"The State says they are not up to cod."

Thinking quickly plus needing a place to live and work, Ralph said, "Would you be up to making a deal?"

"What kind of a deal are we talking about, Sonny?" the old man asked.

"My wife and I are looking for a job, and a place to sleep nights. We're almost out of money. If you let us stay there, we'll fix the places up for you."

"I don't know you. How do I know you are on the level?"

"What do you have to lose? You need the places repaired. We need a place to stay and work?" Ralph said quickly, "Besides, you work right up front here and will be able to keep an eye on the place."

Putting his large, greasy paw to his chin, the man pondered the idea for a few minutes. Then with a smile and a cackle, he said, "Putting it that way, I guess you're right."

His face was friendly, even with the few teeth he had in his mouth

"Good. Could we move in tonight?"

"Sure, but I don't want the Feds after me, so you have to fix yours first."

"That's fine with me.

Ralph extended his hand to the man. The old man took it.

"My name is Ralph, and this is my wife, Vanessa."

"Glad to meet you, Ralph. You to Vanessa," he said, bending to look into the car.

"Vanessa, why don't you go find the cabin you want while I talk to your man?"

"Looks like you have a pretty young woman you married there."

"She is beautiful, isn't she?" Ralph said.

"That sounds like a deal, then," the old man said

Sticking out his grimy hand one more time, Ralph shook it.

"I'll buy what is needed to repair the places. As long as you fix them up to code, I'll feed the two of you and you can stay free."

"You have a deal," Ralph said.

Again, the old man cackled, "By the way, my name is Wayne, Wayne Patterson."

Even as old as the man looked and smelled, Ralph still had an instant liking for the old fellow.

"It's still light enough to see. Want a quick tour?"

"I found the one I want," Vanessa said, rejoining the two men.

"Okay then, let's go."

Wayne gave them a quick tour of the buildings. It was almost too dark at the end of the tour to see anything anyway. It was an eye-opener for Ralph. Wayne led them into and out of the six cabins very quickly. Ralph knew he would have to inspect them again, come morning.

Huge trees and bushes growing around a couple of the cabins hid their cabin from anyone's view. Most of the overgrowth was going to have to be removed. With the tour over, Wayne went back to his garage.

It was dark when Ralph and Vanessa stepped into their cabin. Vanessa had picked it for them. Looking around at the work that had to be done, Ralph's mouth went dry. With hardly any experience, he knew he had a lot to learn in a short time.

So, this is the place Vanessa and Ralph would be calling home.

Although the cabin Ralph and his sister had to stay in was in shambles, it was still better than what they had been living in before.

Taking the flashlight, Ralph went to see Wayne at the station. The old man was sitting at his desk reading a book.

"Wayne, do you have sheets and blankets we could borrow?" Ralph asked him.

"Go on back to your cabin and I'll bring them to you," he said.

As the old man walked into a back room at the station, Ralph once again heard the weird cackle. Taking the sheets, blankets, and pillows from Wayne, Ralph walked back to the cabin. Shining the light on the cabin, Ralph could see the exterior of the cabin was in need of repairs to the roof and a fresh coat of paint. A better estimate of what will be needed will have to be done in the morning.

Inside their cabin, the walls were cracked, dry, and peeling. Sections of the ceiling had dry water spots from the leaky roof. Some ceilings were bulging or hanging lose due to water damage and were ready to fall. From what Ralph could see, he would have to replace all the walls, ceilings, electrical, and plumbing. Of course, that would be after he fixed the outside.

Ralph was too exhausted to start stropping the rooms tonight. In the morning, when he felt more rested, he would start by stripping all the rooms. Five minutes later, Ralph's thinking was interrupted by a knock on the door. Opening the door, Wayne was there with bedding.

Wayne, with old drop cloths, to cover the windows. While Ralph covered the windows and secured the doors, Vanessa cleared cobwebs and swept the place before she made the bed. Exhausted from the last few days, they went to bed.

Once Ralph turned out the lights, they lay quietly in their new bed. In the quiet, even with the windows being covered, sounds of crickets and frogs from a nearby stream gave Ralph and Vanessa a peaceful feeling.

Lying in her usual place against Ralph, with his arm around her shoulders holding her close, Vanessa had a sense of security for the first time in quite a while.

"What is that sweet smell?" Ralph asked.

"It's perfume. I borrowed some from your friend's sister. Do you like it?" she asked.

"Yes, I like it," he said, hugging her. "Maybe once I make some money, I can buy you some."

"That would be super," she squealed, "I like the smell, too."

With a habit of talking in bed, Vanessa's words sounded so grown-up, especially for a girl her age. Even though he was proud of her, he had suppressed his laughed.

"Good night, Vanessa."

"Before we go to sleep, could you give me a kiss?"

"You are my sister, Vanessa, not my wife."

"All I want is a little kiss," she pouted.

To make her happy and to have her be quiet, he rolled to face her. Avoiding her lips, for fear of starting something, he quickly kissed her cheek and rolled back over.

"That wasn't a kiss," she said.

"That is all you get tonight. Good night."

In seconds, they were asleep.

Chapter 13

Early the next morning, Ralph was up before sunrise. As always, Vanessa stayed on her side of the bed, curled up, sound sleeping. Not wanting to wake her, Ralph let her sleep as he made another quick tour of the cabins. Outside, he saw Wayne walking toward the station.

"Good morning, Wayne."

"Hello, young feller," Wayne said, "You and your missy sleep good last night?"

"Very well, thank you. Do you have any coffee?"

"I'll make some right now. Have some doughnuts too, if you want them."

"Sounds good to me, don't mind if I do."

Ralph bit into his doughnut. About to sip his coffee, when he heard his sister hollering for him.

"Ralph! Where are you?"

Quickly stepping outside, Ralph went to the corner of the building and waved.

"I'm here at the station, Vanessa."

Seeing him, she ran to him, grasping him around the waist and laying her head on his chest. She had forgotten her padding.

"You scared me when I couldn't find you," she told him.

"I'm sorry. I wanted to give you some extra sleep."

"I'm awake now."

"Before you come inside, go get your padding on."

"Oh, I'm sorry. I was just so happy to see you, I didn't think."

"No problem. Once you have changed, come back for something to eat."

Ralph watched his sister run back to the cabin. Once she was out of sight, Ralph rejoined Wayne. Wayne was cooking bacon and eggs.

"I'm going to need a huge trash bin, Wayne," Ralph told Wayne as he poured another cup of coffee.

"I'll get you one first thing," he told Ralph.

When Vanessa came into the station, Ralph was amazed at how beautiful she looked.

"Now here is a beautiful gal," Wayne said, smiling at her.

"Thank you, kind sir," she told him, smiling back.

"If you weren't already married and I was a few years younger," Wayne chuckled, "I would marry you myself."

"Now that sounds like a deal."

"Sit and eat," Wayne said, quickly changing the subject.

The food tasted as good as it smelled. They ate seconds. Once they had finished eating, Ralph walked Vanessa back to the cabin and then set to work. A couple of hours later, when Ralph had one of the buildings gutted, two huge trash bins were delivered to the work site.

By the end of the week, with Vanessa's help, they had five of the cabins gutted. Finding water damage in all of them, Ralph let them sit open to dry, while he turned his attentions to his own cabin.

The first room he began to remodel was the kitchen. After tearing out all the old drywall, Ralph diagramed the electrical and plumbing as they now were. He had to be reasonably sure he would be able to put everything back the way it was before.

With the kitchen gutted, Ralph went to Wayne with the list of materials he would need. Wayne first inspected the job, then, taking the time, Wayne took Ralph to the lumberyard. While Ralph was getting the materials needed to do the job, Vanessa took control of the station.

While at the lumberyard, Ralph bought manuals to help him in his endeavor. From that point in time, Wayne gave Ralph an open tab for any materials and tools he would need for the job. With his order loaded on a truck, Ralph returned to the job site. First and foremost, he had to start putting Vanessa's kitchen back in shape.

Anxious to apply his newfound knowledge, Ralph and Vanessa worked until it was too dark to see. Several times that day, Wayne came by to see if they needed anything and to feed them.

Over the next month, piece by piece, room by room, Ralph, with his sister and a new friend named Steve Ralph met at the lumber yard, helped them restore the main cabin to its original self. It seemed as if Wayne was an endless tap, giving Ralph money for whenever he needed it.

Wayne was happy, the way the cabins were beginning to look. He had made a good deal with this young couple, he thought.

Steve Sergeant was the man Ralph met at the lumber yard one day.

"My name is Steve Sergeant. Can I help you?"

Steve was a huge man, but as nice a man as Ralph could hope to meet. Steve had dark hair, an olive complexion, and hazel eyes. He towered over Ralph, standing over six feet and weighing at least two hundred fifty pounds.

"I'm refurbishing five cabins for Wayne. . ."

"I know who he is," Steve said.

After Ralph told Steve what he was trying to accomplish, Steve asked, "How much do you know about the job you're about to get involved with?"

"Not much," Ralph said.

Telling Steve about his life, leaving out being Vanessa's brother, he hoped the man could help him. Finding Ralph an interesting young man, he became interested. Because of Ralph's young age and knowing of Wayne, Steve volunteered his services to help with the renovations when needed. Besides, there was something Steve liked about Ralph that made him want to help, at least to get started on the right path.

"Why don't I come with you to your job site? You can show me what you have done and what it is that you want to do next."

"I'll appreciate any help you can give me," Ralph told him.

Steve's interested in what Ralph was doing was more about curiosity. After that first day, whenever Steve had free time, he would take the time to go to the job site to lend Ralph a hand. To make the job easier for her brother, Vanessa helped by doing small jobs and gopher work.

"Need some help?"

Turning to the voice, Ralph noticed Steve standing in the door watching him work.

"Steve, it's good to see you. What brings you here?"

"Thought I'd drop by to see how you're doing."

"I'm glad. I could use some of your expertise."

"Let's see what you have here."

"Steve, meet my wife, Vanessa. Vanessa, this is Steve, the man from the lumber yard."

"Nice to meet you, Steve. Ralph said you have been very helpful to him," she told him.

"Nice to meet you, too, Vanessa." He said, taking her hand.

CHAPTER 14

Ralph enjoyed Steve's help. He also found he needed all the advice Steve could give him. Seeing the boy needed help, Steve took time off from his work to help Ralph get the good start he needed. It took one month with Steve and Vanessa's help to complete the main building.

On the day the main cabin was completed, Steve invited Ralph and Vanessa to supper at his home to celebrate a job well done.

"Why don't the two of you join my wife, Cathy, and me for supper tonight at our house?" Steve said. "We can celebrate the completion of the beautiful job you did on this building."

"Without your help, I would not have done all this so quickly," Ralph told him.

"We would love to come," Vanessa quickly said, breaking in on her brother's conversation, "But we will need to know how to get to your house."

"A good point," Steve said.

He gave Ralph the directions to his home before he left. That night would be the beginning of a nice relationship.

Never having been to Steve's home, Ralph had a little trouble finding it. Ralph had to take back streets through what seemed to be far out in the countryside. Eventually, they saw the long ranch-style home sitting on a hill not far from the main road.

In all, Ralph had driven eight miles to Steve's home. Pulling into the driveway, Steve and a tall, buxom woman were standing beside the driveway, waiting for them.

"What a beautiful woman," Vanessa said when she first saw Steve's wife. "I would like boobs like that when I'm older."

Getting out of their rusty Chevrolet, Ralph and Vanessa held hands for show as they moved to meet Steve's wife.

"Ralph, Vanessa, I'm so glad you could make it to our home."

Turning to his wife, Steve said, "This is my wife, Cathy. Cathy, this is Ralph and Vanessa, the young couple I've been telling you about."

Taking Cathy's hand in his, Ralph was amazed at how small her hand felt for such a big woman.

For a big woman, she was dainty, he thought.

Cathy was tall, standing a few inches shorter than Ralph. In Ralph's mind, that made her close to six feet tall. He couldn't help but stare at her. Hanging low, to just her shoulders, her medium-length black hair framed her pretty face. Her body frame supported large breasts, rounded hips, and long, solid legs. To Ralph, he could see why Steve would be attracted to her. Not only was she beautiful and sexy, she was also wholesome, outgoing, and very friendly.

"Hello, Ralph." She said, smiling, then turning to Vanessa, she said, "Let's leave the men to talk, while we keep each other company in the kitchen."

"I'd love to," Vanessa said. Vanessa was in awe as she walked into the spacious house.

It would be the first of many times Ralph and Vanessa would spend at the Sergeant's home. Immediately, they felt completely at ease, as if they had known them for years. After dinner, they began talking about their families. Steve and Cathy had been married for twenty-five years and had two daughters, both in medical school.

Ralph gave them a short lie about how they were living. With night over, Ralph and Vanessa bid them good night. On the way back to their cabin, Ralph had a serious talk with his sister.

"Vanessa," Ralph whispered, "we have to tell Steve and Cathy about us."

"What if they try to split us up?"

"Why would they do that?"

"Because they might feel the way we are living is completely wrong."

"I think we have to take that chance. You need to get back to school in the fall, and it isn't fair, or good for that matter, to keep lying to them."

"But I don't want to go away from you, Ralph. I couldn't handle that," Vanessa said.

"No one will take you away from me," Ralph told her. "We belong together."

"I'll go by your decision," Vanessa said, "Just remember, whatever happens, that I love you."

His lying continued to bother Ralph. Back at their cabin, Ralph stopped his sister before they entered the cabin.

"Come here, give me a hug," Ralph said.

Opening his arms to her Vanessa, she flew against him for a giant hug. They stood that way, just holding each other. After a slight kiss on the lips, they parted. Tears were in their eyes.

After going to bed, they quickly fell asleep.

One night at Steve's house, after four months had gone by, Ralph knew they would have to take a chance and confide in Steve and Cathy about their big problem.

Ralph had just turned twenty, Ruth was fourteen near fifteen. Tonight was the night Ralph and Vanessa planned to clean their souls.

"Steve, Cathy, Vanessa, and I have something we have to tell you.

We want to trust you with our secret, because you have both been too good to us. If what we have to tell you go against your beliefs, tell us, and we'll be on our way."

"What could be so bad?" Cathy said.

Ralph told the whole terrible story. Not once did Steve or Cathy interrupt or show any signs of disapproval. Finished with their story, Ralph and Vanessa waited for a response. Silence filled the room for what seemed to be forever, when it was really only a few seconds.

"Is that all?" Steve said.

"Yes."

"Even though it was wrong, Cathy and I understand why you did what you did. We don't condone what you did, but we're both proud of you for the guts you displayed and your fortitude. We're both proud to know such fine people."

"Thank you," squeaked Vanessa through tears.

"You are the biggest surprise, Vanessa. We didn't think you were eighteen, but we had no idea you were only fourteen."

"How old, did you think I was?"

"We thought sixteen or seventeen, because of your maturity."

Everyone talked further on the subject. The answer was the same. Vanessa had to finish school. To solve that problem, Vanessa would leave the cottage early each morning, come to Steve and Cathy's home, where she would become a child again. At night, when returning from school, she would again pretend to be Ralph's wife. Though Steve and Cathy didn't like the idea of the masquerade, they went along with it to show their support.

"How do the two of you sleep?" Cathy asked.

"Together," Vanessa told her.

"Isn't that a little dangerous?" Cathy said.

"If you mean sexually, then no," Vanessa said. "We have been sleeping together ever since I was born. Speaking for myself, I like it that way."

"But you're turning into a beautiful young lady; you need your privacy," Cathy said.

"We have no secrets," Vanessa said.

"Are you telling us you see each other nude?" Steve said.

"What's the big deal? Married people see each other all the time."

"Yes, but the two of you are not married. You're brother and sister."

"In my heart were more than brother and sister," Vanessa told her. Their eyes never wavered.

"That's not a healthy way to think," Cathy said.

"We're not having sex, and never will, but we need each other for strength, especially at night," Vanessa said.

"What do you have to say about that, Ralph?"

"I have to agree with Vanessa on that issue, but I must admit it does have difficult moments."

"Well, we have no say in the matter, but because we trust both of you to do right, nothing will be said to anyone by us."

"Thank you, we appreciate it," Ralph said.

With Steve's help, a second cabin was finished. They would start on number three in the morning.

When school started, Cathy enrolled Vanessa in the nearby school as an adopted daughter, using Steve's address to keep their secret alive.

Steve Sergeant, at forty-six years of age, is a huge man, with a powerful upper body and sturdy legs. He and Cathy, who is forty-four, have two daughters. Both girls are in medical school. Sherry, their oldest, is twenty-three, while Harmony is twenty-one.

Steve has worked for the lumberyard since his graduation from high school. Starting as a helper in the yards, Steve worked his way to supervisor when the man who held the job retired. Now assistant manager, Steve had the ability to take time off any time he wished without worry of losing his job.

Cathy is a big woman who stands a solid five-foot-eleven. Her body supports extra-large breasts and long, muscular legs. She has chestnut hair, which is cut short. Her hair frames her pretty, round face with horn-rimmed glasses. Cathy has been one of the lucky women, being able to stay at home with her children. Her home is always clean, and food is always on the table when her husband gets home.

Steve first met Cathy at a church function, where both were very active as kids, dating casually at first. Later, when they knew they couldn't live without the other, they married. Two years later, Sherry came into the world. Cathy was a natural mother. Almost two years to the day that Harmony was born.

Steve first built a small home on a hill just outside of town. When Cathy became pregnant, Steve and Cathy decided to remodel.

CHAPTER 15

Sherry, Steve, and Cathy's oldest daughter was in her senior year at medical school. Once school was behind her, Sherry had plans to settle with her practice in the area where her parents lived and she grew up.

Sherry is a beautiful young woman with her mother's body and her father's looks. The only difference between mother and daughter is their height. While Cathy stands five feet eleven, while Sherry stands only five feet one. She is the only short person in the family.

Harmony, her sister, is tall like their parents, but wasn't as endowed with a body as her mother or sister. That was always a sore spot for Harmony. Harmony had always thought she had been cheated and resented her sister for it.

Throughout high school, Sherry dated casually, but never had any thoughts about getting serious. Sherry had to finish medical school before she could think of raising a family. After graduating high school, she said goodbye to all her friends and proudly left for medical school.

For her first five years, while in medical school, Sherry devoted all her time to study and received honors. In her sixth year, she dated for the first time. Wanting her parents to be proud of her, she refrained from having sex. As far as Sherry knew, she was the only twenty-three-year-old virgin in the school.

It wasn't until her senior year of medical school, Sherry allowed herself to date a fellow student named Michael Long. Michael was the person who would change her way of thinking. In fact, he made her leery of all men. From her experience with Michael, she didn't have any desire to marry.

They met one day while in the library studying for an upcoming exam. Sherry glanced up from her notes for just an instant to rest her eyes. Sitting across from her was a very handsome young man. It had been so long since she had actually dated. She wasn't counting the few boys she had in the last few years. The boys she dated, those few times, meant nothing to her except as an escort for the night.

There was something about the man across the table that made her keep glancing in his direction. At first, he seemed to be ignoring her. Sherry made it a point to talk to him. When she broke silence, she noticed he was reading the same textbook she was.

"Excuse me," she said.

Putting down his book, he acted annoyed. Giving her a blank stare, she nearly wished she had disturbed him. Once he saw the pretty face of the young woman sitting across from him, who was trying to talk to him, he softened and smiled at her.

"Are you speaking to me?" he asked, acting stupid.

"Yes. I see we are studying the same text."

"Is that unusual?"

"No, but if we studied together, wouldn't the assignment would be easier," she said.

"You could be right. Shall we give it a try?"

"First, I need to know your name."

"That would be helpful," he chuckled, "My name is Michael, Michael Long."

"It's nice to meet you, Michael. I'm Sherry Sergeant. Now that we have the introductions out of the way, why not continue our conversation at the café down the street?"

That seemed to be the beginning of a long relationship. They met at every chance, at first just to study together. After the third time together, Michael asked Sherry for an actual date.

"Why don't we make a date for supper sometime?" he said.

"That would be nice, but I really can't afford extras yet," she told him.

"I'll buy. After all, I did ask you."

"I couldn't let you do that," she said

"I insist."

"Can you afford it?"

"Yes, of course."

Afraid of asking more questions, Sherry accepted his invitation.

For the next six months, they studied every day. Friday nights, they went to supper at an expensive restaurant.

Wining and dining women always came easy to Michael. He always won over any girl he wanted, with his money, looks, and charm. One Friday evening, while dining in one of Michael's expensive haunts, he gave her a ring.

"I would like it if you would wear this ring," he said, quietly holding the box out for her to take.

"Oh, Michael, it's so beautiful. Are you asking me to be engaged to you?" she asked.

"Yes."

"Yes, oh yes, I was hoping you would ask me."

Finals were creeping up on them. Sherry was falling in love for the first time in her life. She didn't stop to consider why she was falling so quickly, after not dating for so long. Getting to know each other better would have been the better choice. She thought he felt the same.

Michael had given her every indication his feelings were genuine.

Letting her guard down, after a nice dinner and dancing one night, she finally went to bed with him. A virgin, she cried the first time, not because of the pain, but for the beauty of the act itself. She had never dreamed sex could feel so good.

The engagement lasted just until after their graduation ceremony. Once Michael had accomplished his mission and the finals were over, he broke the engagement.

"Sherry, I have something to tell you." He said, one night as they lay in her bed.

They had just finished making love. His arms were still around her, cuddling her as she came down from her high. Her head was resting on his chest, listening to his heart beating. She was thinking, is this what Mom and Dad feel when they are together in bed?

"I'm listening."

"Do you know Donna Johnson? She is the girl in our chemistry class."

"What about her?"

"She's pregnant."

"Oh no," Sherry said, "She must feel awful being she's only a junior. She'll miss the rest of her schooling."

"That's not all of it."

"There's more?"

"Yes. The child is mine."

"Yours?" Sherry said.

Quickly disengaging from him, she was out of the bed and out of his reach before he could say another word. Turning to face him, she felt humiliated, used, and terribly hurt. She didn't want to look at him, but there were questions she wanted answers to.

"When did this happen?"

"Remember the night you didn't feel well and went to bed early?" he said.

Sherry knew instantly what he was going to say. Disgusted and feeling dirty, Sherry moved quickly to get into her clothing. Michael continued to lie in the bed. He had a nasty grin on his face. His only regret was losing such a delectable creature.

Sherry was by far more beautiful and sexier than Donna ever thought of being, but Donna was new, and Michael enjoys every new relationship.

As Sherry hurriedly dressed, she began to feel sorry for Donna. She would only last a few months like all the other girls, she thought. Michael never really loved any of the women he bedded. He uses them as a tally. How many new women will he get? How many virgins will he break? He had the gall to tell her, there had been seven virgins, since the girl named Shelly, he had in high school.

"You couldn't wait for me to feel better?"

"Let's just say, I didn't want to wait. Donna and I wanted each other, and we did what came naturally."

"You are a bastard. How could you do this to me?"

"You did it to yourself."

"Don't you blame this on me?"

"If you weren't so stubborn, we could have had sex without all these promises and games."

"Get the hell out of here, and out of my life, you lowlife bastard."

By the time Michael had gotten out of bed and was putting on his clothes, Sherry was on her way to the door.

"Before you go, let me say, sex with you has been great, and I will miss it."

Stopping instantly, she turned and quickly retraced her steps.

"Are you saying you only slept with me because I was available?"

"You weren't easy to land, but the wait was worth it. You are a spectacular lay."

"You are a rotten bastard, and I hope you fry in hell. I gave you my virginity and you are making fun of it," she said

Slapping him across the face added fuel to the fire. The sound of the slap was a sharp pop. It left a red handprint on his cheek. Wanting to hurt her mentally, he let the slap fuel him further. Laughing at her, he left the room without looking back at her. He left the door wide open in his wake.

Chapter 16

Harmony, the youngest daughter in the Sargent family, two years younger than her sister, has two more years to finish medical school, after her sister had graduates.

In her own eyes, having always been in competition with Sherry her whole life, she wanted to prove to everyone, most of all to herself, that she was as good or better than her sister. Harmony's wish was to follow her sister's example to become a doctor. A better doctor than her sister would ever be.

She took after her father's side of the family with a long, lanky body. Harmony was also jealous of her sister's larger breasts and rounded hips. In her own eyes, she looked basically too skinny and hard-looking compared to Sherry, who had the soft and curvy, feminine look.

Though she didn't believe it, Harmony was beautiful in her own way, but that was never good enough for her. Harmony blamed Sherry for all her downfalls. Her hair was longer than her sisters and had a natural curl to it, which Harmony hated. Sherry's hair looked softer, not as scraggly.

Harmony had, in her own eyes, a boy's body with slim hips and skinny, yet muscular thighs. Sherry had rounded hips like their mother and fuller, sexier thighs. That made Sherry look more like a woman and not a boy like Harmony. Trying to compete with her sister at an early age was very difficult. In her eyes, she would never match her older sister. A deep jealousy of Sherry always got Harmony into trouble in her younger years.

Harmony constantly blamed her sister for her bad behavior and misfortune. At the early age of fourteen, Harmony instigated a liaison with Danny Howitzer. Danny was eighteen and the older brother of Harmony's best friend, Suzy. The break came when Suzy went to the store for her mother. Harmony took advantage of Danny, who was in the other room watching television.

"I have to go to the store," Suzy said. "Do you want to go with me?"

"No, I think I'll stay here and bug your brother."

"That ought to be interesting," Suzy said.

As Suzy went out the door, Harmony estimated the walk would take at least one and a half hours. Harmony didn't waste a second.

"Hi Danny, how have you been doing?"

Never taking his eyes off the television, he said, "Without."

Suddenly, Harmony's mouth went dry. She was about to do something she had been wanting to do for some time now. This was the perfect opportunity.

"If you pay attention to me, maybe I can help you out."

Immediately, Danny looked at her.

"Harmony, if you were older and had a woman's body, I might think about it."

"How often do you get a chance at having a virgin?"

"You're still a virgin?"

"Yes, and if you're nice to me, I'll give it to you."

"Where is Suzy?"

"She had to go to the store."

"When did she go?"

"Two minutes ago."

"All right, you want it, I'll give it to you," he said, coming off the couch. "Do you at least have tits?"

Harmony swallowed the lump in her throat as she took off her blouse. She had tits, but they were small. Having gone this far, she didn't stop there. As quickly as she could, she got out of the rest of her clothes. Standing naked in front of him, she blushed. His eyes felt as if they were burning her skin. As he stared at her naked body, he licked his lips.

"Come and get it," Harmony told him.

Going to the couch, Harmony laid back, giving him a good view of what she was offering him. In seconds, Danny was out of his clothes and on top of her.

"Seeing we don't have much time, this is going to be quick," he told her.

Harmony felt him push against her. Then she felt a slight pain. The pain made her realize what she was doing. Panicking, Harmony changed her mind. Before she could push Danny away, he thrust. In an instant, he had fully penetrated her. Once inside her virgin body, his actions were quick. In seconds, he was finished.

Returning early from the store, Susy walked into the living room and stopped. The sight of Danny mounting her best friend froze her. In that same instant, Danny climaxed, pushing himself deep inside Harmony. Harmony's legs were wide open, and she was moaning. The way her head was swishing on the couch cushions, it was obvious Harmony was enjoying the romp.

"What the fuck?" Suzy shouted. "You fucking whore. I leave for a second, and I catch you screwing my brother. Get out of my house. Our friendship is ended."

Laughing from embarrassment, Harmony scrambled off the couch. Suddenly embarrassed, Danny shot to his feet. Everyone looked down at the couch cushion, only to see the blood stain that had left its mark. Nervously picking up her panties, Harmony slid them on.

By the time Harmony had finished dressing, Danny had already dressed. His attitude was, so what. He was sitting back in his chair, watching the screen.

"Thanks for the initiation," Harmony spat, as she went out the door.

Hearing Suzy shout at Danny made her laugh.

"How could you fuck her?" Harmony heard Suzy say, "She was my best friend. Now you have ruined that."

"Relax, Suzy, she initiated it."

The last Harmony heard was Suzy saying, "Well, you had better figure out how to get the blood out of the couch before Mom comes home."

Harmony's life and attitude changed after that. From that time on, she took what she wanted, from whom she wanted, whenever she wanted. It was the way she wanted to live her life.

Over the next two years, Harmony became the school whore, laying down for any guy that would take her out. In those two years, Harmony became pregnant twice. After two abortions, before the age of sixteen, she blamed the men for not wearing a rubber.

The first pregnancy was the result of a one-time romp in the back seat of an old Ford with a senior from her high school. Wanting notoriety, Harmony got it when she let Brad have her. Brad, being the captain of the football team and a senior, gave her what she wanted. He was a tall, burly young man with blond hair and a fast reputation. Chasing him became costly.

One night after a home game, after everyone else was gone, Brad took her behind the school to have sex with her on the ground. It was the only time she had sex with him. From that time on, Harmony built a reputation of being easy.

Wanting nothing else to do with Harmony, Brad tried avoiding her. Word quickly got around to that effect. He would laugh about what an easy lay she was. Two months later, Harmony told him she was pregnant. Confronting him on the football field in front of everyone embarrassed him.

"You're going to be a daddy, Brad. I'm pregnant."

"Are you sure?" he said.

"It has been two months, and I went to the doctors."

"How do you know it is mine?" he said, "I am sure I am not the only guy you had between those legs."

"You are the last boy I have been with."

"You're a slut, and we only did it once, two months ago," he growled at her. "How many different guys have you screwed in the last two months?"

"None, you were my last," she lied.

Brad had made two mistakes. His first mistake was to have sex with her. His second was in laughing at her. Enraged at being laughed at, Harmony charged him with raping her. Having had sex with most of the young men on the football team, at one time or another, Harmony couldn't prove rape.

Still, by starting rumors, Brad received a lot of bad publicity. That publicity hurt him. With only one choice left, Brad transferred to his uncle's home to let the publicity die down. Moving to his uncle's home in another state would give him a fresh start.

Chapter 17

Harmony's second pregnancy came a year later. To earn extra money, Harmony began babysitting for some friends of the family. The man she was babysitting for knew of her reputation. One night after he and his wife came home, Sam Gastonia decided he wanted a little for himself.

Every time she babysat for the family, Samuel, the twenty-seven-year-old father of the baby, made it a point to drive her home. Liking Sam, she was willing to have a little sex with him if he wanted to. Being he was married and finding the man sexy, she knew he had to be experienced.

From the beginning, the drives home were just talk. She knew that by always agreeing with him, she would be able to pump his ego. Many times, she would appear at a store or some other place when she knew he was there alone. Sam never suspected Harmony of stalking him. He always took the time to be nice, which spurred her on.

Then came the night when Sam came back early, because his wife had become sick. As soon as they got home, Sam put his wife to bed. Knowing Harmony was downstairs and waiting for him to drive her home, Sam knew he had the opportunity he had been waiting for. To ensure he wouldn't be missed, Sam gave his wife two sleeping pills to make her sleep.

That night, on the drive home, Harmony gave him a little push. Sitting closer to him than usual, she let her thigh touch his. From his reactions, she knew she was winning. Because of the sleeping pills Sam gave his wife, he would have plenty of time to go as far as Harmony would let him.

Harmony has been egging me on, asking for it. Sam doubted she would turn me down. He had to make his play for her. As Sam came downstairs, he saw that Harmony was still there. Sam was hoping she would still be there. Seeing her, Sam smiled to himself. This was the night he might be lucky. Not only was she looking so sexy in her blue jeans and light-yellow sweater, but she was actually giving him the sign she wanted him.

"Ready to go?" he asked her.

"Ready when you are," she told him.

As they walked together to the car, Sam could feel the heat radiating from her body, and he wasn't even touching her. On the drive to her home, Sam didn't have an idea how he was going to approach her. Wanting to impress her with his ability to handle women, he remained quiet. Pulling up in front of her house, Sam cut the engine and turned off the lights. His senses told him she was ready. His first hint, she didn't try to get out of the car as soon as he stopped. On the previous trips, he knew she was waiting to see what he was going to do.

Shifting in his seat, Sam turned to face her. In doing so, he placed his arm on the back of the seat. Where he placed his arm, it was lightly touching her shoulder. Being extremely nervous, he looked into her eyes. Another hint came when she shifted on the seat to face him. She didn't move away when his hand touched her shoulder.

Harmony knew from the way he was acting that he wanted to say something, but didn't know how. Not wanting this opportunity to escape her, she turned to face him. Moving in the seat as she did, the way she placed her leg, she knew he could see her panties.

Wanting to know how she felt, Sam tried looking into her eyes. He was now more nervous because of the way she turned to face him. Her eyes were now in the shadows. Sam knew Harmony was actually too young, but knowing her reputation, he was willing to take this monumental chance.

Yes, she was young, but she was so sexy and so tempting. Sam knew she was inviting him. She had the ability to turn him on every time they met. He knew she was waiting for him to make the first move.

His mind was betraying him, especially the way she was facing him. He couldn't help but look at her crotch, covered only by her panties. He needed to say something before it was too late.

"Your house looks dark. Aren't your parents' home?" he said in a cracked voice.

"No, they're on a night out with some of Dad's clients, and my sister is at a girlfriend's house for the night."

"Well then, we can't have you staying alone in that big house. I'll go in with you, if you would like me too."

"I'd like that. You're a nice man. Being with you is fun," she said, knowing his intention.

"I won't be able to stay too long. As you know, my wife is sick in bed. If we take too long and she does wake up, I won't know what to tell her."

"Try telling the truth. Tell her why you stayed," Harmony told him, in the sexiest voice she could muster.

"I couldn't do that."

"I don't mean the real reason. Tell her because my parents weren't home and you wanted to be sure I was safe."

"That should work. Maybe, I should call and tell her."

"Don't do that. She might get the wrong idea. If she asks when you get home, bend the truth. Meanwhile, let's go inside and get comfortable."

Getting out of the car, Sam followed Harmony to the door. The movement of her slim hips spurred him on. He liked the idea of slim hips instead of the large, fat ones his wife sported. Ever since their kid was born, her body has gotten out of shape. Hell, Harmony was larger in the chest than Shelly. Shelly didn't have much more than pimples from the beginning.

As soon as they entered the front door, Sam couldn't wait any longer. Pulling her close, she came to him willingly. Turning her face up to his, she kissed him, quickly sliding her tongue into his mouth. Immediately, Sam's ardor rose. Soon, they were grappling with each other. Both were starved for sex. Sam used the excuse because his wife was pregnant again, and Harmony because she was Harmony.

"God, Harmony, I need you," Sam said.

"I need you too," she panted.

"My wife hates sex when she is pregnant," he lied. Actuality, her ardor was higher. "She is always telling me it's too uncomfortable for her," he lied again.

"Take me to bed," Harmony whispered to him.

By the time they reached the bedroom, their clothes made a path directly to the first bed they came to. Starting in the living room, with no preliminaries or protection, they had a quick start and a hasty ending. The feel of her tight vagina around his pulsing erection was enough to cause him to have a quick release. Sam wasn't surprised that Harmony wasn't a virgin. He did, however, find that sex with her was overpowering, leaving him with wanting more.

For Harmony, the sexual trip went too quickly. Every time, the man she was with would leave her crying for more. None of the men knew how to stimulate her enough to satisfy her. She hoped that one day she would find the one man to make her happy.

Harmony had Sam hooked. She would call him whenever she felt like having some fun. Her hooks were into him. Being under her control as he was only made him hate himself. They continued having sex every chance they had for the next six months. One night, trouble reared its ugly head. It was the night, while Sam's wife was upstairs with the kids, Harmony dropped the bomb.

"I am pregnant, Sam."

"Jesus Christ, couldn't you have been more careful?"

"Careful? Me? You're the one who can't keep his pecker in his pants," she told him.

"You little bitch, what do you want from me now?"

"I was hoping you would divorce your wife and marry me."

"Aren't you a little young to be married?"

"I am almost sixteen."

"You're only fifteen! Jesus Christ, I thought you were older."

"Surprise, I am nothing but jail bait."

Quietly, Sam paid for her abortion, then quickly moved out of town. Sam was a lucky man; his wife or the law never found out about Sam's affair with a minor.

Having two abortions didn't stop Harmony from continuing with her sexual tirades. She just became more careful in her sexual practices. Using countless lovers, the rest of the way through high school and while in college.

Harmony's only ambition was to hurt her sister. Her jealousy of Sherry was overpowering. Even worse, Sherry had no idea of her sister's plan. Harmony figured the best way to hurt her sister would be to seduce her sister's husband, if she ever married.

After her trial marriage to Michael, getting Sherry to marry will probably be a long time coming. She giggled at the thought.

Harmony was on campus when the news of her sister spread like wildfire. In one way, she felt sorry for Sherry, knowing how she must feel. On the other hand, maybe she deserved it for being such a smug person.

For her own feelings and wanting to know what type a lover her sister would pick, Harmony made it a point to meet Michael. Meeting with Michael, she had to make it seem incidental. She had to be sure, whoever he was, Harmony didn't want him to know Sherry was her sister. To get even with him for Sherry, after she got what she was after, she would tell him who she was.

Once she had Michael's interest, Harmony knew it would be easy to get Michael in bed. It didn't take long, as she suspected. He was already tiring of his latest girlfriend. In bed, Harmony found Michael a good lover. But he was too much like her. Knowing how she felt, Harmony doubted Michael would ever find happiness.

Harmony would have to wait patiently for the day Sherry got married. She would also have to be sure that once she was finished with medical school, she would become her sister's partner. Working with Sherry would make it easy enough to betray her, once she got the chance.

Chapter 18

For the next two years, everything went as planned for everyone. At fifteen, Vanessa went into her sophomore year in high school. Ralph was proud of her achievements and her honor roll status.

Ralph, with Steve and Vanessa's help, finished renovating the last of the cabins. Tomorrow, Wayne would make his inspection tour. Ralph knew his work would pass.

"You did a great job here, Ralph," Wayne said, "You are a handy kid to have around."

"Thanks, Wayne, I appreciate that."

"How would the two of you like to stay here, free rent and manage the cabins for me?"

"You're not kidding, I hope."

"Not on your life," Wayne chuckled. "Is it a deal?"

"It's definitely a deal," Ralph said, shaking Wayne's hand.

That evening, when Vanessa got home from school, Ralph gave her the good news. The next time they had dinner with Steve and Cathy, they passed on the news.

One night, a few days later, while the four were enjoying supper and conversation, a beautiful woman Ralph had never seen before came into the room. Since opening her clinic, Sherry had little time to spend with her family. On this particular night, she surprised everyone with a surprise visit.

"I hope you have a place set for me?" Sherry said, coming through the door.

"Sherry. You made it. Your father and I were wondering when you would find the time to grace us with your presents," Cathy said, getting up from the table.

Ralph's heart nearly stopped. The woman who walked into the room was extremely beautiful. He found he couldn't take his eyes off her. The resemblance was there, making Ralph sure the woman was Cathy's daughter. She was even more beautiful than her mother, but much shorter.

Scanning the woman's figure, Ralph could not help but notice how much slimmer her hips were than her mother's and how small her waist looked than that of her mother. The only place the woman matched her mother was in the bust line. With hair, russet in color, hanging loosely around her shoulders, it highlighted her flawless olive complexion. Out of all the women he has met, she was the first woman to hold his attention.

Unable to help mind, Ralph watched Sherry intently as she talked. She always held the eyes of everyone she talked to. Instantly aware that the woman wasn't very interested in anyone other than her mother and father. Ralph's heart sank with disappointment as they were introduced.

"Sherry, I want you to meet two nice young people. We have come to like very much. This is Ralph and his sister Vanessa. They live in town and manage the newly built motel for Wayne Patterson."

"Hi Vanessa," Sherry said, with a smile.

Turning to Ralph addressed him coldly. Her attitude toward him made him question himself. Did he say something to make her dislike him? Even so, Ralph had a hard time forgetting her.

To stir his attention away from Sherry, Ralph and Steve talked about work and fishing. Ralph kept an ear open to what the girls were saying. He found that Sherry was three years older than he was.

Chapter 19

Another two years passed, and Harmony came home as planned. Sherry didn't have a clue that her sister had so much hatred toward her. Ignorant of the fact, Sherry allowed her sister to become a limited partner in the clinic.

Another two years sped by with both sisters working side by side. Their camaraderie was growing, and they seemed to get along better than they ever had. Neither of the two sisters was married nor had any plans to do so in the near future. Harmony was too intent on waiting for Sherry to get married to be serious with just one man. Besides, why marry the bull when you get more sex without marriage.

Whenever Harmony dated Sherry would always be on call at the clinic. Harmony never had a chance to meet Ralph. She was too busy most of the time, yet she had heard plenty about him from Sherry.

"When are you going to introduce me to your new love?" Harmony said one day at the clinic.

"He is not my love. We just see each other now and then when he and his sister are at Mom and Dad's."

"You don't date, do you?" her sister asked.

"No, I'm not comfortable with him or any man, for that matter. Besides, he is three years younger than I am."

"More my age, I guess," Harmony said, trying to see what reaction her sister would come back with.

"Why don't you leave him alone, Harmony? You have more than

enough studs to keep you happy." Sherry said sharply.

"Now, now, let's not get catty. Are you jealous?"

"I'm not jealous," Sherry said, with a laugh.

"Do you know Sherry? I think you need a little sex in your life. How long has it been since you had a man?"

"That, my dear sister, is none of your damn business."

"Oh, bull shit, if sisters can't confide in each other, they have problems."

Harmony wanted very much to meet the man, especially if the two were becoming serious. Once she got on his good side, it would be easier to seduce him, if he ever married Sherry.

"If you must know, it's been more than seven years."

"Jesus Christ, Sherry, you're too young to give up on the best part of life. Christ, I hope when I'm twenty-nine, I don't dry up like you have. How do you do it? If I couldn't haul some guy's ashes now and then, I'd become stark raving mad."

"Christ, Harmony, you've had more men than a porcupine has quills. How are you ever going to find a man to settle with? Don't men satisfy you, or are you some kind of a nympho?"

"Oh, my sister can hit below the belt," Harmony said, laughing.

Vanessa had been spending a lot of time with Cathy. She saw Cathy as a mother figure. Cathy was the mother; she never had, even though her brother did just fine in keeping her happy and content.

The first time Vanessa met Harmony, she took an immediate dislike to her. She didn't know what bothered her about Harmony, other than the fact that she was sneaky and a whore. There was something in Harmony's manner that made Vanessa not to trust her.

Sherry was different from her sister in many ways. It was difficult to believe they were actually sisters. Sherry would be the type of woman she would want for her brother. In fact, Vanessa hoped Sherry would be her sister-in-law someday, even if she is a few years older than her brother.

Vanessa could see her brother slowly falling in love with Sherry, though he didn't believe he was. She wished she could get Sherry to see her brother as the person he really is. If she did, Sherry would see Ralph differently.

Sherry told Vanessa about her history in school while they were having lunch one day. Now, Vanessa understood why Sherry acted as she did toward Ralph. Meeting Sherry for lunch was becoming a habit for Vanessa. She looked at Sherry as an older sister, a sister she had so many times yearned for.

A couple of times, Harmony asked Vanessa to join her for lunch. Not liking or trusting Harmony, she never accepted the invitations. Vanessa was the kind of person who didn't care if Harmony knew she didn't like her.

One warm summer day, when the cabins were full of occupants and the maintenance was complete, Ralph approached Wayne on another subject.

"Hey Wayne, I am going fishing. I need a rest."

"What if someone wants a room?" Wayne said.

"We're all full, besides, you can do it for me, for a little while, can't you?"

"Sure, have fun and catch some for me."

"I will. See you later."

At twenty-six, Ralph had grown into a huge man with wild, good looks. There were plenty of girls in town who had an interest in him, but Ralph didn't have time for dating. He loved his work, and the time he spent by himself fishing was more than satisfying. Ralph was content with his lifestyle. Sure, he missed sex, but other than that, Vanessa gave him everything else any man would want; she gave him love and affection.

"Later," Wayne said, going back into the garage.

At his apartment, Ralph donned his bathing suit and packed a lunch. Knowing Wayne loved fish, if he caught any, he would be sure to save them for Wayne.

Since graduating from high school, Vanessa and Cathy started a small business of their own. They baked goods and sold them from the house. The arrangement was good for both of them. If either of them wanted time off for any reason, they took it? Knowing the other could always hold down the fort was nice.

At twenty, Vanessa had grown into quite a beautiful woman. Taller than Sherry but shorter than Cathy, Vanessa had grown into a sexy body. Her light brown hair, which she constantly wore in a ponytail, looked very rich and silky. It even felt silky, at night, when she lay in her brother's arms to sleep.

Figuring Vanessa would spend most of her time with Cathy, something his sister has been doing a lot lately, Ralph decided to go fishing alone.

Getting into his old jalopy, Ralph headed for his favorite spot. It was an island he saw when traveling to this town. He had found the island was better than he thought, quite by accident. Remembering the island and looking for a place to get lost. On that day, he had driven halfway through the canyon to the island he had always wanted to explore.

Driving at a slow speed, Ralph saw what he thought was a small opening in the side of the mountain. Stopping in the first available spot, Ralph drove back to the spot. With no one behind him, he turned into the open space. The space was tight, but he made it through. As he assumed, there was enough room to park his vehicle and turn around.

CHAPTER 20

The walls of the canyon were steep on each side of the gorge. Almost barren, sparse amounts of brush lined the walls. The sparse vegetation provided little shade. The river and road wound like a ribbon for thirty miles through the canyon. From the canyon, the river flowed fifteen miles, flowing between two small towns, then emptied into the ocean.

Several small wooded islands sitting in the center of the river lay scattered through the canyon. Most of the islands in the river were tiny, more like sand flats, at low tide in the ocean. Only one looked like it afforded the privacy for someone wanting to get away. That particular island also looked difficult to get to.

From the road, after crawling over the guard railing, Ralph clung to the guard rail as he positioned himself to make the drop into the water below. The drop was only a foot or so, but he didn't know how deep the water was.

From above, the shallow water looked deeper than it really was. Most people wouldn't care to venture to the island, figuring it wouldn't be worth the risk. Ralph, on the other hand, was determined to get to the island even if he had to swim.

Dropping into the place he wanted, he was mildly surprised to find the water only came to his knees. Wading the fifty feet to the island itself was easier than he had anticipated.

Once past the shallow section of the river, Ralph found a path hidden from view on the road. The path led through a dense wooded area to a small, sandy beach on the other side. The beach sat at the edge of a large, cool, clear pond, fifteen to twenty feet in diameter. Hidden from tourist eyes, it seemed like an ideal place where he could bathe in the nude.

Ralph was surprised at the serenity of the place. Traffic noises seemed to float overhead, leaving only the sound of the rushing water cascading over rocks. The pond was filled by a small waterfall from the main river. It was plain to see that only those who dare venture to the island would get to know how peaceful and quiet it was there. From seeing the torrents on the far side of the island, it was difficult to see how the water slowed so quickly, to form pools, then continue in torrents, once it left the safety of the island.

Over the years, the swift action of the water cut away portions of the rocky mountain, leaving in its wake a deep pool. A small overhang covered a calm area for swimming. Worn smooth by years of wear, a rocky ledge four feet below the falls allowed the water to trickle slowly into the deep pool. Another source feeding the pond had to come from underground springs, which made the pond icy cold.

From the road, Ralph could see why tourists would think the rushing water flowing through craggy rocks at each end of the island was all there was to the river.

Below the larger pond was yet another smaller pond. A shallow waterfall, fifteen feet wide and eight inches deep, allowed the water to slowly fill the second pool. From that point, the water picked up speed again, giving the pretense of being nothing but rapids.

It was at that private pool that Ralph accidentally met Sherry one Sunday afternoon. That meeting would change their lives forever. Although Ralph and Sherry had seen each other several times, at her parents' home, neither thought the other person was serious enough to start a close relationship.

Sherry respected Ralph for what he had done and continued to do for his younger sister. Also, he had always treated her like a lady, never attempting to come onto her. That impression she got from him was that he wanted her friendship. That suited Sherry fine.

Still leery from her encounter in college, she was happy that that was all Ralph wanted. Yet there was something about him that made her want to know him better. A thought suddenly popped into her head. A thought she didn't know she was capable of. Maybe he would be willing to have a small affair with her. God knows she needed a man in my life. She wasn't getting any younger.

CHAPTER 21

At twenty-nine, Sherry was just three years older than Ralph. Their age difference didn't seem to matter much for a casual fling. As far as she could, Ralph was a nice guy, and her parents trusted him. That was enough to get her thinking. Vanessa, Ralph's sister, was all ready like a sister to her. Maybe Vanessa could give Ralph a sign, she is interested in him.

Ralph enjoyed just being around Sherry, just looking at her. She was beginning to enjoy his stares, but didn't dare try anything, for fear of losing any chance he might have later.

Playing it cool, Ralph wanted to see what Sherry wanted out of any relationship they could have. He would love for the two of them to have a meaningful affair, but he didn't have the nerve to try anything.

Besides, there are Steve and Cathy to think about. They probably would be very angry with him were they to find him sleeping with their daughter, without the benefit of marriage. Ralph didn't want to lose their friendship. If something were going to happen between him and Sherry, it would have to be spontaneous.

The day everything changed in their lives was a warm, quiet day. Ralph had gone fishing and was lying on the small sandy beach a few feet from where his fishing line entered the water. It was almost noon. Fishing for almost three hours, Ralph had caught three large German Browns. He intended to have them for supper tomorrow night.

Lying where a small ray of sunlight filtered through the tree branches, he began to feel sleepy. The filtered rays gave him a little shade along with enough sunlight to keep him warm.

Relaxing near the water, he suddenly heard the snap of a twig behind him. Alert, but lying still, Ralph turned his head slightly. He needed to see what sort of animal would be coming through the wood. Perhaps a deer or something had found its way there. He had been coming to this spot for two years now and had never encountered any other human.

In the next instant, to his surprise, Sherry, bending low to avoid the low-hanging branches, came into view. Once she was through the coverage, she stood to straighten her swimsuit. A branch had caught the bra of her bikini, nearly baring a large breast. A look of surprise was cast upon her pretty face when she saw Ralph staring at the breast, nearly hanging out of her bra.

Ralph had often wondered what Sherry would look like nude or in a bathing suit. Now, before him was his answer. Sherry was wearing a pale blue string bikini that showed off her slim hips, which gave definition to her tiny waist. Sherry was to Ralph's perfection at its highest. The bikini also showed off her muscular legs, but didn't hide too much of the rest of her body. Her flowing russet hair, bunched on top of her head, was held in place by a comb, making her look years younger than her twenty-nine years.

Why would such a beautiful woman hide such a beautiful body under such baggy clothes? The first time he saw her, he knew she was extremely beautiful, but he had no idea how utterly beautiful she really was until this moment.

"Oh, Ralph," she said in surprise, "I didn't know you knew of this island."

"It seems that two of us do now," he uttered.

Turning to leave, she said, "You were here first. I'll just leave."

"No, don't go," he said quickly, "I'd like to know you better, and as far as I know, this isn't a private pool."

"How much better do you want to know me?" She gasped.

"As much as you will allow me too," he told her with a grin.

"That could be dangerous," she said, chuckling with nervousness.

"Also, fun," he added, "How about you stay and we talk?"

"If you promise to be a gentleman," she said teasingly.

"Haven't I always acted like a gentleman with you?"

"Yes, but I've always had more clothes on. I need to know you will be more of a gentleman now that I'm dressed as I am."

"I'll try," Ralph said teasing back.

Both began laughing in the same instant. After adjusting her bikini, she leaned over she spread her towel in the sand near the edge of the pool. Her bikini top was so tiny that it had trouble containing very much of her large breasts. Both nearly came into full view. He almost got a view of her nipples as she bent over to spread her towel. Her breasts, coming out of her bikini top, didn't seem to bother her. What impressed Ralph most was her natural beauty. Once Sherry was settled on her towel, Ralph lay back in the sand to talk.

Ralph had to interrupt her twice, each time to land another fish. Having caught his limit, he placed the fish on a gut line through the fish's gills, then laid them back in the water to keep them alive. Now he was able to give his full attention to Sherry. They talked a while longer until she excused herself.

"I'm a little warm," she said, "I think I'll take a dip."

As soon as Sherry got up from her towel, Ralph couldn't help but admire her grace. The movement of her slim hips was a turn-on. To make matters worse, she walked to the edge of the pool, and the movement of her soft, round butt cheeks stirred his blood.

Stepping onto the rock ledge at the deep end of the pool, Sherry poised herself before diving in. Before diving, she looked at him and smiled. Her agility was apparent as she cut the water with hardly a splash.

Surfacing, she had to smooth back the hair away from her face. Even with her hair pulled back, she was as beautiful as ever. In his eyes, nothing could mar her beauty. He was already in love with her and didn't realize it.

With short, quick strokes, Sherry swam to the left side of the pool near the waterfall. There, the water flowed gently into the pond. Reaching up, she grabbed the ledge. She began climbing the rocky edge, only to sit beneath the falling water as she reached the falls. Gaining her balance, she stood. Raised her arms, she spread her thighs and lowered her head to allow the water to cascade over every inch of her exquisite body.

At that moment, Ralph wanted nothing more than to be near her, to touch her. Walking to the edge of the pool, where she had been a moment sooner, Ralph made his dive deeper than Sherry did. Coming up, Ralph was startled to find her treading water close in front of him. Face to face, inches away from her, he desperately wanted to kiss her. The smile on Sherry's beautiful face stole his heart.

From her perch under the cascading water, Sherry watched Ralph dive into the pool. The image of his muscular body and handsome face made her shiver with the thoughts of being held in his arms.

In an instant, she made her decision. Ralph would either kiss her or turn her away. At that moment, to get her answer, she would have to be brazen and give him the signal. Knowing his dive was deeper than hers. In a quick decision, she dove into the pool to meet him before he could surface. Treading water, she waited for him to emerge. When he broke the water, they were in the center of the pool together. Both were treading water inches apart. Their eyes send the message. Without a word, they slowly moved to shallow ground.

Now, able to touch solid ground, they stood as close together as possible without touching. Willing the other to begin, they moved the same instant, as if a pair of hands was pulling them together. Without hesitation, their lips touched softly, just barely for an instant. As if it were wrong, bewildered, they pulled away from each other just for a few seconds. With hearts pounding in their chests, they could do nothing but stare at each other.

Remembering the feel of her soft lips pressing against his, Ralph suddenly felt humble. At that moment, Ralph said to himself, what he wouldn't give for a lifetime of those kisses.

His lips are like a heated fire, Sherry thought. Once touched, she knew it was what she wanted forever. The sensation of the first kiss drew their lips back for a second kiss.

Like pouring fuel to a flame, the second kiss washed all thoughts of right and wrong away. Only desire remained. They needed to be devoured by the other. A gnawing sensation drew them together with an unquenchable hunger. Instantly, they reached for the other. As if it were a natural thing to do, they came together in a kiss that seared their souls.

Hotter than either of the first two kisses, their last kiss lasted longer than normal. An irresistible heat was generated between them. Neither understood what had happened, nor did they care.

"I don't know what's happening to me," she said.

Her breath was coming in short spasms.

"Me either," he moaned.

"I've never spontaneously kissed a man like this before, let alone a man I hardly know."

"Nor have I, especially with such a beautiful woman. I had no idea I would ever have a chance with a woman like you."

Had she heard him, or was she ignoring his comment? In reality, his kiss drew her into a void. All Sherry could think of was his lips on hers. Not able to resist being apart, their lips met again. This time their kiss was sweeter and deeper than any kiss they had ever known.

"My God, that kiss was so great," she moaned.

Laying her head against his chest, she sighed.

Ralph was careful not to become too insistent. Suddenly feeling a chill, they moved toward the bank. For all the time they had been standing in the water, the cold finally got to them. The heat their bodies generated wasn't enough to keep them warm any longer. Hand in hand, they emerged from the pool.

Enraptured, they sat in the sand, close together, staring deeply into the others' eyes. Lost in the rapture of love, they neither wanted nor needed time to go by so quickly. They wanted time to stand still. They wanted to enjoy this moment forever. Now, all the fears and distrust they felt before melted away. Both knew they could love and trust again, as long as they were together.

CHAPTER 22

Just as the sun was setting below the trees, shadows colored the area black. Ralph pulled his Chevy into his parking space behind his cabin. After climbing from his car, Ralph lifted his catch, wrapped in paper, lying on the floorboard by the front seat.

It was a great catch. Switching on the light behind the cabin, Ralph lay the fish on the man-made counter. Immediately beginning the cleaning process, he threw the gutted fish into the deep sink and the guts into a pale under the sink. After preparing the fish to eat, Ralph washed them thoroughly before wrapping them in freezer paper.

With the fish clean and wrapped, he washed his hands again before entering the cabin. Opening the door to the cabin, he stepped inside. Vanessa was at the stove, but didn't turn to greet him. She was busy cooking. By the sweet smell of herbs and spices filling the cabin, Ralph knew Vanessa was preparing chicken for dinner.

Taking off his shoes, Ralph slid past her to put the fish into the freezer. Another aroma filled his nostrils. Glancing around the room, he spied a pie sitting on the counter. With the table set for two, Ralph knew Vanessa had missed him. Walking up behind her, he placed his arms around her waist and kissed her neck.

"I'll give you four hours to stop that," she said, shivering in rapture.

Laughing, Ralph said, "Everything smells so great."

"It's something I've been working on to surprise you," she said.

"Where did you learn to cook like this?" Ralph asked, hugging her closer to him. Suddenly, the image of Sherry popped into his head. This is what he wanted to do with Sherry, not his sister.

"Cathy taught me," she replied.

Releasing her, Ralph moved to the counter where Vanessa had a platter of chicken already cooked. Picking up a wing, he gnawed on it. Vanessa didn't admonish him for sneaking a piece of chicken. Pleased, she smiled.

"The chicken is just the way you like it," she told him, "I also hope you like the pie."

"If it tastes as good as it smells, I know it will be delicious."

Giggling, Vanessa returned the favor by coming up behind him as he nibbled the chicken and hugged him.

"You're almost as good as a wife."

"What do you mean, almost?"

"You cook well, you clean house good, and you make me happy except in one way," Ralph said, with a smile on his face.

"What way is that?"

"No sex."

"I am sorry about that, I wish I could help you out," she teased back.

"Don't be Vanessa. It is just the way it has to be."

"I know," she sighed, "I wish it didn't, but it does."

After washing his hands a third time, Ralph sat at the table waiting for his sister to join him. After setting the food on the table, Vanessa took her seat across from him. Reaching for her brother's hands, she said, "Can we say grace?"

"I think that is a good idea."

He took her offered hands in his. Vanessa said the prayer Cathy had taught her. Even though the food was delicious, Ralph had no appetite. His mind drifted into overtime. All his thoughts were of Sherry. The feelings he was having for her were taking hold. He never dreamed that he, a common laborer, would have a chance with the beautiful young doctor. It was hard for him to imagine, especially since Sherry is three years older. How could a doctor have feelings for him, as he has for her.

Noticing her brother wasn't eating, she asked,

Startled, Ralph quickly looked up at his sister, "I am fine, Vanessa, really, I am."

"You're acting as if you're a million miles away."

"Sherry was at the fishing hole today," he whispered, "while I was fishing."

They talked as Ralph ate. Later, he helped her clear the table, wash the dishes, and put them away. As they were preparing for bed, Ralph glanced at his sister. Used to seeing Vanessa nude, it never occurred to him before how much her body has changed. When they first arrived in this town and she was using padding to give her age. Ralph never thought about her to be a woman. Now the curves he was seeing were all hers and natural.

Thinking back, he couldn't remember the last time she had worn the padded body parts. Now, at twenty, Vanessa had turned into a full-grown woman. She didn't need padding any longer. Her breasts, not large, were big for her petite size. Her hips were full and curvy, and her waist was small.

His eyes took in the rest of her lingering at the junction between two full muscular thighs. The junction he stared at was full of light brown hair, the same as was piled on her beautiful head. For the first time, he was beginning too realized just how beautiful his sister really was. Her face was that of an adult, not the skinny kid.

When they slipped into bed and Ralph turned out the lights, the room plunged into darkness. Only a sliver of light from the moon shining through the window cut a beam across the bed. Feeling

Vanessa lying next to him instantly brought thoughts of Sherry rushing through his head. Is this what it would be like if it were Sherry lying next to him in bed? Seconds later, the awareness of his sister's looks hit him.

This was Vanessa, not Sherry, the woman he wanted in bed with him. The fact that they were still sleeping naked together never bothered him before, because he had seen her as a kid. But now, his sister was a full-grown woman.

Ralph tried to shake off his negative feelings. Vanessa wasn't the woman he should have feelings for. With wild thoughts filling his head, Ralph found he couldn't relax. How could he tell Vanessa, without hurting her feelings, that they could no longer sleep together naked?

As always, just before they fell asleep, Vanessa would roll against him and throw an arm around his waist. Then he thought about his arm, which lay across her pillow, around her shoulders. It was a ritual they had done for many years, since they were kids.

CHAPTER 23

Every night, for the last fourteen years, he had cuddled with his sister. They took comfort from each other. Now, for the second time, Ralph was painfully aware of Vanessa's firm, soft, bare breasts pressing tightly against his side. Instantly, panic set in. He didn't want to think about the nature of his feelings, about the stirring in his groin. Now, with an erection, he knew he had no choice.

Quickly, before he changed his mind, Ralph gently pushed her away from him. Sitting straight up in the bed, his sudden movement startled his sister. Coming to her knees, she let the covers drop around her. She was now kneeling directly in the beam of moonlight, giving Ralph a great view. Seeing her with his wide-open eyes, he knew he was making the right decision.

"What's wrong, Ralph?" Vanessa asked.

"This arrangement has to change," he said.

"What arrangement?"

"The two of us sleeping in one bed, naked together," he said.

"Why are you saying this? What has changed your mind?"

"You have changed. Your body has changed, and I am having feelings I shouldn't."

Now, to make matters worse, Vanessa was kneeling naked on the bed facing him. With the bed covers removed, her ample, firm breasts and narrow hips were uncovered. His eyes automatically dropped to the shadow between her thighs. The sight of her youthful body put lurid thoughts into his head. They were thoughts he shouldn't be having. He also knew if she remained in this bed tonight, the night would end in disaster.

All day long, his thoughts have been on Sherry. He liked those thoughts. Now, seeing Vanessa like this fully disarmed him. Worried about his feelings for his sister, he failed to realize his body was now uncovered as well.

It was the look his sister gave him and the words she mentioned that brought him to reality. Vanessa's eyes stared for the first time at his huge erection.

"My God, you are big down there."

Embarrassed, Ralph quickly covered himself.

"This is what happens when a man and a beautiful, sexy woman like yourself go to bed naked together," he said.

"It has never happened before," she said.

"Until tonight, I never realized how beautiful you are."

"You didn't think I was beautiful before?"

"You were a kid before. Now, seeing you have turned into such a beautiful woman, everything has changed."

"What does that have to do with us sleeping together, as we always have?"

"You are so desirable, I get urges for you I shouldn't be having."

"I know, I've been having urges lately too."

"Because we are brother and sister, wanting each other is wrong. Not doing anything about those urges goes against the laws of nature."

"If we weren't brother and sister, what would you feel?"

"I wouldn't be sitting here like this talking about it."

"It's too bad we're brother and sister, then."

"Seeing you like this, I have to agree," he said.

"What would you like me to do?"

"Come with me. I'll help you make the bed in the other room. That is where I will be sleeping from now on."

"I wish we didn't have to sleep alone. I'm going to miss you not being with me, comforting me when I need you."

"I'm going to miss you more than you realize, Vanessa," he sighed, "but this is the way it has to be from now on."

Still hard, Ralph slid from the bed to slip into his shorts. Finding them on the floor, next to the bed, he bent to retrieve them. After putting them on, he turned and saw her smiling.

"What's so funny?" he asked.

"Your thing is still standing straight up, and it bobs as you move."

"You're not supposed to be watching me."

"Why not, you look at me?"

Suddenly feeling naked, Vanessa slipped into a large T-shirt that covered most of her mature body. Ralph was relieved she was now covered. Sadly, Vanessa followed her brother into the room across the hall.

Once across the hall, as his sister bent over to make the bed, Ralph got a glimpse of the backs of her calves, thighs, and pubic hair, as the garment rode up from behind. The outlines of her cute bottom made him want to touch her, to caress her, fondle her, and lastly take her to bed and have his way with her.

I have to stop having these thoughts, he thought.

Quickly moving to the other side of the bed, Ralph continued helping her make the bed. As Ralph turned down the sheets so he could get into the bed, she lifted the shirt over her head. Once again, his eyes fastened on the ripe flesh in front of him. Holding his breath, he waited until she left the room before sliding into bed.

Back in the other bedroom, when Vanessa climbed into the bed alone, she began to cry. This bed was now cold. Sitting with the covers on her lap, she cried.

The next morning, as was her habit, she walked into the kitchen naked. The sight of her naked body was difficult for Ralph.

"Vanessa, we have to stop being nude in front of each other. Seeing you naked as you are is driving me crazy," Ralph told her.

"Seeing you, as I did back there in the bedroom, didn't help me much either," she told him.

"That's why this sleeping arrangement is better for both of us."

"Maybe so, but I'm going to miss your warmth next to me at night, or when I can't get to sleep."

"I'm going to miss you, too."

Just before her brother left the room, Vanessa pulled the covers up to her chin, covering her young breasts from his view. Now that she was covered, he began to feel a little more relaxed.

"I love you, Ralph," he heard her say.

"I love you too, Vanessa, very much," he told her.

Closing her bedroom door behind him, he crossed the hall to his now lonely bedroom.

Back in his own bed, Ralph felt lonesome and cold without Vanessa lying next to him. Turning out the light, he found that sleep would not come easily for him.

Chapter 24

The next morning, when Ralph dragged himself out of bed, he felt tired and depressed. After taking a shower, he didn't feel much better. Not feeling as good as he should, he knew what the problem was. He would have to get used to it.

Vanessa was already in the kitchen making breakfast when he walked in. She turned toward him as he entered the room.

"I hope you slept better than I did last night," she said.

"Not too good, I missed you too?"

Vanessa enjoyed working in her new kitchen. Ralph had put in extra cupboards and counters, a new electric stove, a dishwasher, and new florescent lights that made the kitchen seem bigger and brighter.

"Would like some breakfast before I go to work?" Vanessa asked.

"Breakfast would be nice, thanks."

Admiring his work, Ralph kept thinking about all he had left to do. All that remained was to hook up to the sewer line from the garage sewer line, and they would be off septic use.

Besides hooking the sewer line to the main line, painting all the rooms was all they had left to finish. As far as the painting, Vanessa insisted she be the one to pick the colors, promising not to get too gaudy.

After breakfast, Vanessa joined Cathy at her home to work. Ralph stood outside and admired the work he and his help had accomplished. Now that all the cabins were rehabilitated and full, Ralph ached for something else to do. Just managing the cottages didn't seem to keep him busy enough.

With a new idea brewing in his mind, Ralph approached Wayne. Finding Wayne in the garage office watching television, he confronted him.

"Wayne," Ralph said, bursting into the office.

"Jesus Christ. You scared the shit out of me," Wayne said, springing out of his chair.

"I was wondering what that smell was," Ralph chuckled.

"You are so funny," Wayne said, "What do you have?"

"I'd like to build four new cabins, behind the existing cabins," he said, "There is a lot of property still not being used. With more cabins, you would make more money."

"What is your idea?" Wayne asked.

Taking out some sketches he had been working on, Ralph showed Wayne what he proposed. Nervously, Ralph paced as he waited for Wayne to make a decision.

"Think, we could rent them?" Wayne asked.

"Sure, we don't have enough cabins now," Ralph replied.

"Okay, then do it."

Jumping into his jalopy, Ralph drove to the lumberyard to confront Steven. Confronting Steve, Ralph told him what he proposed. Before going back to the cabins, Ralph stopped at City Hall to get permits. Ralph was told it would be the first of next week, before the Surveyors would be there.

Back at the site, Ralph marked the area where he wanted the new cabins to be sitting. As soon as the permits were in his hand and the site was surveyed, he would contract a crew for site preparation. Once the sites were ready for the buildings to be built, he would start working on the four new cabins.

One night, by the end of the week, Ralph, totally exhausted, went to bed early. Vanessa had stayed up to watch her favorite programs. Sleep came hard for her, too. Not having her brother to cuddle with, she felt alone.

Sometime during the night, Ralph awoke to go to the bathroom. Still, groggy with sleep, he fell back into bed and instantly fell back into a deep sleep.

Hearing her brother up, Vanessa listened until all was quiet. Missing him terribly, Vanessa quietly moved to his room. Needing his warmth and comfort, she slid into the bed next to him. Because he was asleep, he wouldn't know she was sleeping with him until morning when he woke up. After all, she was a grown twenty-year-old woman who should be able to keep things under control.

Ralph's dreams were erotic. In his dream, he was living in New York, in a penthouse on the thirteenth floor. After a date, Sherry had come back to the apartment with him. They had a few drinks and danced to slow music. The mood was light, yet both knew what was going to happen before the night was over. In the middle of a dance, they stopped and looked into each other's eyes. Words need not have been spoken.

While Ralph turned out the lights, pulled the drapes, and locked the doors, Sherry went to the bedroom to undress. The apartment was warm. Having had more to drink than she should have, she was ready for anything. After getting naked, she pulled down the covers and then slid into bed to wait for him. Taking longer than she thought he should, she laid back to rest her eyes.

Going into the bedroom and seeing her with her eyes closed, he thought she had fallen asleep waiting for him. Not wanting to disturb her, he undressed and climbed into the bed next to her. After turning out the lights, he lie quietly listening to her shallow breathing, thinking of what might have been.

Needing to hold her, he rolled toward her. Fitting her sleeping body to his, he looped an arm over her slim waist, pulling her closer to his body. With her lying so tightly against him, he could smell the sweet aroma of her body.

To his delight, she parted her thighs, allowing his thigh to slide between hers. She must have felt his erection pressing against her buttocks. Instantly, she began wiggling her rounded buttocks against his raging desire. It did nothing but heighten his desire for her.

In the back of his mind, he vaguely remembered the smell of her perfume. In his sleep-drugged-erotic mode, he swept it from his mind. Drifting deeper into his dream, he began to let his hands roam over her body. Deep in his mind, he could feel her garments between them. Reaching below the hem of her garment, he let his hand rest on her velvet thigh. Removing his thigh for better access, he started moving his hand slowly upward.

Feeling no resistance, he let his hand move tantalizingly slowly up her thigh to her rounded buttocks. Still feeling no resistance, he slowly enjoyed the feel of her bottom. It felt warm, soft, and erotic. Expecting resistance, but not getting any, he moved his hand over her hip to her flat belly. Feeling her stir, he began a slow, rubbing motion just above her pubic hair.

When Vanessa slid into bed with Ralph, she laid quietly to be sure he was asleep. Turning on her side, she curled up to sleep. Suddenly, her eyes popped open. Feeling him mold himself to her backside, she bit her lip, lest she utter a moan. Wanting to tease him, she wiggled back into him as she used to do when she was younger. The action gave her food for thought. Instantly, she felt his erection press into her buttocks.

Daring, Vanessa lifted a thigh to allow him access for his thigh to slide between hers. The feeling was wild. It threatened to bring her out of her sleepy mode. Suddenly, his hand began moving downward. Then, as his hand moved up again under the hem of her gown, she sucked in a gulp of air. His hand now lay on the bare skin of her thigh close to her crotch. She had all she could do to lie still.

Though she felt him remove his thigh from between hers, his hand remained where it was. The feel was so exciting. In seconds, his hand began moving ever so slowly upward. Liking the way his hand felt, she let out a sigh and closed her thighs to trap his hand in place.

Even though her thighs were closed, it didn't stop him. He moved higher until it was cupping her soft bottom. He felt so warm, strong, and dangerously tempting that she decided to see what he had in mind.

Slowly, his hand moved over her hip to her flat belly. Her insides began churning. The soothing touch of his hands rubbing her belly just above her pubic hair began to excite her further. As her breathing deepened, she felt her throat go dry. Instead of relaxing, she was becoming overheated. Feelings she had never felt before made her want more, yet those feelings confused her.

Slowly, his free hand moved softly upward to capture and caress her breast. Instantly, her brain told her that what was going on had gone far enough. Her brain was telling her to stop him, but the pleasure her body was receiving overrode the warning signs her brain was sending her.

Painfully slow, his hand moved upon her breast before slipping beneath the fabric. As his open palm grazed over her nipple, she gasped with pleasure. Feeling his fingers tweak the nipple, a ferocious shock wave shot through her. Never had anyone ever touched her like this before. Soon, she was floating with the pleasure her body was receiving. The pleasure was doing things inside her that she never knew existed. She was quickly losing control.

The sensations were so delicious, she didn't want him to stop. As his hand kept massaging her bare breast, she lost control. Realization of what was about to happen suddenly broke. Her first thought was to get out of bed. Realization of why he told her not to sleep with him suddenly hit her. At first, she thought he was just teasing her. Now she knew things had gone past the teasing part.

Instead of getting out of bed as she should have done, she turned to face him. His mouth had taken the place of his fingers. His tongue began circling her nipple, while his teeth tenderly nipped on it.

The hand that had been kneading her breast had now slid down over her body to her pubic hair. At this time, his hand slid between her thighs. Unable to stop herself from the pleasure she was receiving, she lifted her thigh, allowing his hand to cup her there. With his hand at her crotch, she knew she had lost.

Ralph's mind was churning, directing his actions. Instantly, his hand moved to her breast. It felt so soft and yet firm. Taking a nipple between his finger and thumb, he tweaked it. Her reaction was wild. Massaging her breast a few moments longer, he became surprised when she turned to face him. Without waiting any longer, he took her breast into his mouth. He licked and nipped the same nipple while his hands moved downward to the junction between her thighs.

Automatically, her thighs opened, allowing him access to her most intimate part. As his hand moved over her vagina, feeling dampness, he knew he was going to make love with her.

Suddenly, with a scream, Vanessa came back to reality. Quickly, she moved away from his seeking hands. Her sudden movement woke him.

"What?" Ralph uttered, trying to gain some composure.

"I am so sorry, Ralph. I know now I should not have come to your bed. But missing you so terribly, I couldn't stop myself," she sobbed, frightened.

"Vanessa?" he said, still not sure what was going on. "What were you thinking?"

"I wanted to feel you near me again," she sobbed.

"I told you before, this wouldn't work."

"Everything was fine, even when you were feeling my breast."

"That should have never happened," he told her sharply.

"Your hands felt good on me. What scared me was your erection rubbing against my thigh. I was afraid you were going to get on top of me. If you did, I wouldn't have been able to stop you or wanted you to stop," she said.

"Nothing happened, did it?"

"No, I moved away when I felt it. Why did it do that?"

"My dreams were of Sherry."

"Have you already slept with her?"

"No, not yet, but I'm sure we will eventually."

"Do you love her?"

"Very much, but I don't know if she really loves me."

"Believe me, she does."

"How would you know?"

"We're together a lot, and you're all she talks about," Vanessa said.

She quickly moved out of his bed. Once out of bed, she bent, retrieved her nightgown, and put it on.

Ralph watched her as she got out of bed. When she bent over for her nightgown, he could clearly see the breasts he had just massaged. As she slipped the gown over her head, he got a view of the light hair between her mature thighs, the hair he had just run his fingers through. Everything about her was ripe for the taking, and he had passed it up.

With her gown on, Vanessa quickly left the room. Hearing the door slam, he knew she had gone back to her own bed.

Thank God," he sighed, after she left his room, "she is covered. Ralph knew he had been in a very vulnerable position at that moment. If she were to pursue this venture any further, he wasn't too sure he could have kept her away.

When she was gone and the door was closed, he closed his eyes and thanked the Lord that he didn't get the chance to do what he wanted to do.

Chapter 25

It was the next time Ralph and Sherry were at the island, alone at the pool, that nature took its course. They had planned to meet early that morning, at the grocery store parking lot, then go to the island.

As Ralph pulled in, he saw Sherry getting towels and other things for their planned picnic from the trunk of her car.

Pulling in beside her car, Ralph cut the engine. Getting out of his car, he moved to help her. When they met at the back of his car, he took the bundles from her. As he was placing them in the trunk of his car, he became aware of her nearness.

After placing the stool in his truck, he stood. Turning to find her still standing a scant inch away, he boldly took her in his arms and kissed her. There was no struggle. He also relaxed when he didn't get any stiffening, only surrender. She began to kiss him back with a fever.

Noticeably flustered, Sherry emitted a deep moan as she pushed away from him. With her hands going to her lips, she quickly moved back to her red mustang, where she rolled up the windows and locked the doors.

Coming back to him, she changed the subject. The look on her face and in her eyes told him she wanted him as much as he wanted her.

"Did you do the work on this car?" she asked.

Opening the door, she slid inside.

"Yes, but it isn't finished yet."

"I can see it needs a paint job, but the work looks good."

"Thank you."

"You're entirely welcome. I know good work when I see it."

Once both were in the car, refraining from more hungry kisses, he drove off. The drive took forty minutes to get where they wanted to go. Neither of them talked very much during the drive. Nervousness, over what they were feeling, made the mood somber. Once he pulled into his favorite hiding place, he unloaded the trunk, then he locked the car.

It took both of them to carry all the things Sherry had packed to the guardrail. It was a short walk to the river. He wanted to take her hand to safely lead her across the street. Sherry liked the feel of this man when he took charge.

At the railing, he helped her over, then aided her by dropping her into the shallow water below. Once she was steady, Ralph handed her the goods, then dropped down to be with her. Standing next to her, he took the articles from her.

Side by side, they waded through the shallows to the edge of the trees on the island. From there, following the short dirt path through the low-lying branches, they emerged at the small beach on the other side. It had been a chore carting the blankets and picnic baskets, but I felt it was worth the effort in the end.

Even though there was sexual energy in the air, the day started out as the picnic they came for. Ralph spread the blanket in the sand, then placed the basket, with all the goodies, next to it. Settling on the blanket, Sherry quickly laid out a snack, with small sandwiches and soft drinks.

Suddenly, she could feel the heat and love in the air. Neither were able to nibble at the food. Even though they weren't hungry for the food, they sat nibbling while staring into each other's eyes. Both knew, before the day was over the inevitable was going to happen.

This is ridiculous, Sherry thought. I'm a thirty-year-old woman, in love with the man facing me, and I'm afraid to approach him about making love to me.

Ralph's heart was beating so fast, he was surprised Sherry couldn't hear it. Ralph wanted to hold and kiss her so badly he couldn't think straight. Afraid because of what she went through before she met him, he didn't want to scare her off. He was twenty-seven for Christ's sake, why didn't he have the strength to go for it and show her how he felt about her?

After their small snack, which they hardly ate, Sherry stood. Reaching for Ralph, she pulled him to his feet. Just the touch of her hands in his felt like touching a branding iron. Instead of showing him she wanted to be kissed as he hoped, she surprised him a second time by leading him to the ledge overhanging the pool.

Standing close together, holding hands, they were feeling like two teenagers, embarking on something neither should be doing. Not wanting to let go of the other's hand, images of the last time they were together, in this same place, flashed between them. They stood in the same place, waiting for the other to make the first move.

Before entering the pool, they turned to face each other one more time. Longingly, they searched the others' eyes. Before they could stop themselves, their lips touched lightly. Small moans were emitted from their throats simultaneously. A spark erupted between them, seemingly burning their lips. Needing to control the situation and cool down, they dove, cutting the water at the same instant.

Sufficing, they came together again, unable to stay apart. Even the cold water couldn't cool down the feelings they were feeling. Throwing modesty to the wind, they shed their bathing suits, tossing them onto the ledge nearby. Naked, Ralph took Sherry by the waist and pulled her tightly against him.

"It's been a long time, Ralph," she said in husky words.

He didn't comment, knowing the touch of his body to hers told the story. Desperate desire soared between them. In their minds, there was no doubt how this was going to end. Their lips and hands became bolder. In the water, she was buoyant.

Placing his hands under her bottom, he lifted her. Wrapping her legs around his waist and feeling his hardness pressed against her, she reached between them. Grasping him, Sherry placed him where she needed him the most.

Ralph knew Sherry wasn't a virgin. Knowing, he was amazed how tight she felt as he moved deeply into her depths. With escalated passion being so high, the action ended too quickly. Feeling somewhat satisfied, they moved back to the blanket. All thoughts of swimming evaporated.

After coming out of the pool, neither left the other's side. Lying next to each other on the blanket, they began stroking and kissing. Their first time was hot, heavy, and quick; they knew, but that didn't stop them from pursuing a second time. After all the kisses and fondling, they were at each other again. To them, this was the most natural thing in the world to do.

After their second coupling, which was soft and tender, they were fully satisfied. Content and comfortable with each other, they went for another swim.

Spending the entire day together felt natural, as if they were born to be together. The day wore down quickly. As the sun began to set, they suddenly realized, their whole day was gone. It was time to leave their Eden.

"Before today, it had been seven years for me," Sherry told him, lying in his arms. "Now, I want you one more time before we go."

Making love a third time that day, on the blanket, on their beautiful island, was perfect. The act was slow and loving, like they had been together for years. After, as they readied themselves to go back home, Ralph opened his heart to her.

"I think I fell in love with you, the first time I saw you, at your parents' house," he told her.

"I felt something too, but because of my bad experience, I wasn't sure I wanted to try again. Between the way you acted around me and your sister, I was willing to have an affair, to test my feelings."

"After what we just experienced, are you still afraid of me?"

"No, I'm not, but give it some time, Ralph. I'm almost sure, how you feel about me is how I feel about you, too?"

"What is it you're not sure of?"

"You know I've been hurt before," she said sadly, "That is all I'm going to say at this time."

CHAPTER 26

For the next three months, they met at her apartment. The weather had driven them indoors. Each session was as heated as the first and better than the last. They couldn't get enough of each other. Most of the time when they met, they hadn't planned on making love.

Finding themselves alone together, neither of them could keep their hands off the other, so it just happened. It was during one of those times, the two of them, so caught up in their feelings, forgot about safe sex. Two months later, after making love, Sherry dropped her bomb.

"I'm pregnant, Ralph."

"Are you sure?"

His answer scared her. It reminded her of the first experience she had with Michael. She wasn't pregnant at that time.

"I'm a doctor, remember?"

A huge smile broke onto his face.

"I love you, Sherry."

"I love you, too, Ralph," she sighed in relief. "Because this had happened to me before, I was so afraid you didn't love me and were just using me as Michael did."

"Marry me, Sherry."

"Say that again, I don't think I heard you correctly."

"Sherry, the woman of my life, would you do me the honor of

marrying me?

"Do you really mean it?"

"I never meant anything more in my life."

"Oh my God, yes, yes, a thousand times, but please don't hurt me, Ralph, "I couldn't take it."

"You talk as if you don't believe me."

"That's because I was hurt once by the one man I was engaged to before you."

"I know that story, and I don't care. You are my love."

Nodding her head, she then said, "I'm sorry, I don't mean to keep bringing that up."

"I'm sorry, too, but you have to remember, I'm not the other man."

"I know you're not," she said as tears clouded her eyes, "So my answer again is yes."

"Yes, what?"

"Yes, I'll marry you."

"You really want to marry me?"

"Why does that surprise you?"

"Because you're so much older than I am and you're a professional, while I'm not."

"To begin with, I am only three years older than you, and that is nothing. Second of all, what does my being in a professional position have to do with anything?"

"Well, you're smarter and will be supporting the family more than me."

"Let's get something straight, Ralph," Sherry said, "What makes you think I am smarter than you are, because I am a doctor?"

"Well, yes," He said, "I don't want people thinking you married in a lower class."

"I don't give a damn about class. I'm a doctor because I want to help people, not for anything other reason."

"I am afraid you will think less of me, because you will have to support me."

"Will it bother you if I bring home more money than you?"

"No, but I'm afraid it would bother you some day."

"Ralph, I love you for the person you are not, what for what you can give me."

"Do you know, I never thought I would ever have a chance with a woman like you."

"Did you think I was already married?"

"No, because if you were, I doubt you would ever be here with anyone but your husband."

"What a nice thing to say."

"I'm only telling the truth."

That night, Ralph, Vanessa, Sherry, and Harmony were sitting around the table at the Sergeant's house for supper. Just before the prayer, Ralph stood, pulling Sherry with him, holding hands.

"Steve, Cathy, Vanessa, Harmony, Sherry, and I want to tell you our news at the same time. Sherry has agreed to marry me, with your permission."

"I couldn't want a better man for my daughter," Steve said, standing and saluting with his drink.

"We second that," both Cathy and Vanessa said.

"I hope the two of you will be happy together," Harmony said. Smiling. She wasn't smiling for her sister, but because her sister just put her in Harmony's hands. It will be fun seducing this man, Harmony thought, as congratulations were issued around the table.

"So, this means Vanessa will be moving in with us," Steve said jokingly.

"What do you mean, move in with you?" Ralph asked.

"We want to replace the daughter we lost to you. Besides, why would you want another woman around when you have a wife to make you happy?" Steve joked.

"I guess that's fair," Ralph relented. "After all, we are like part of the family anyway."

Steve burst out laughing, "Would you believe I not only didn't lose my daughter but I gained a son, and another daughter in the process?"

"Three weeks from now, the wedding will be taking place at the family church," Sherry announced.

"Vanessa, would you be my matron of honor?"

"What about Harmony?" Vanessa asked.

"I want you," Sherry said, "Will you?"

"Of course, I will. I will be honored," Vanessa replied.

Time flew by, and the wedding was at hand. Radiantly, Sherry walked down the aisle on the arm of her father. At the altar, Steve gave his daughter away, then took his place next to Ralph as best man. Harmony and two girlfriends from her past were also in the wedding.

Steve, not only was he giving the bride away, but he was also to be the best man. Wayne, who also stood up for Ralph, was so happy to be part of the wedding had a complete makeover. No one recognized Wayne as he walked into the church.

After the wedding, Harmony set her plans in motion. At the reception, after Ralph and Sherry had their customary dance, Harmony collared him.

"All right, Brother-in-law, you are mine for the next two dances," Harmony said, moving into his arms.

"I hear the two of you are going to Hawaii for a couple of weeks?"

"Yes, I can hardly wait," Ralph told her.

"I hope you get her pregnant while you're there."

"Why do you say that?"

"Because everyone knows how much Sherry wants a baby," Harmony told him.

"I'll work at it," he said, not telling her that the deed was already done. Twenty minutes later, after excusing themselves from the reception, Ralph and Sherry made their way to the airport.

Chapter 27

After Ralph and Sherry returned from their honeymoon, it was back to the old grind. The only difference, they now had each other to come home to. Time passed quickly, as the baby grew inside her. Sherry did realize the feelings a woman got from carrying a child.

She knew there was a lot of pain involved, but she also knew once the baby was born, the pain would be gone. Now the baby was due in two weeks. Ralph gave up his job at the cabins because he needed more time to take care of his new family. Steve got him a job with him at the lumberyard.

"Now that the baby is due, I will have to stay home with him for a while," Sherry said.

"What about your practice?" Ralph said.

"Don't worry about that, Sherry," Harmony said, "I can handle the clinic until you get back."

"By the way, business has been booming, so I had to hire two new doctors."

"You could have consulted with me first, Harmony," Sherry said angrily, "I'm sure they are good doctors, but I want to be the one to hire and fire."

"I didn't think I had to," Harmony said, getting a little defensive, "the business it is partly my business, too."

"You don't, but it would have been nice to be informed of what's going on beforehand."

"Well, now you know," Harmony said, "besides, this will allow you more time to be home with your baby and give me more time for visitation."

"Under those circumstances, I forgive you," Sherry said.

One night, a few weeks later, as they lay sleeping, Sherry was awakened by sharp pains in her womb. Lying there a moment, she counted the times between labor pains. She knew she had to get to the hospital. Her labor pains were escalating quickly.

"Ralph, Ralph, it's time," she said, shaking him.

"What, what's the matter?" He stammered, still half asleep.

"The baby is coming."

"Oh, shit, why didn't you tell me?"

"I just did."

Flying out of bed, Ralph grabbed the suitcase lying near the door. It was at that moment, Ralph realized he had to help Sherry to the car, but only after he hurriedly put some clothes on.

Ten minutes later, Ralph had Sherry in the car and was on the way to the hospital. On the way, Ralph called Harmony on the car phone. Harmony could hear her sister moaning in the background.

Arriving at the hospital, before them Harmony informed the hospital staff that her sister was on her way in to have her baby. As Ralph pulled in at an emergency room exit, two orderlies with a Gurney came out the door. Sherry was put on the Gurney and wheeled inside. Because of Harmony, Sherry was immediately placed in a room by herself.

While Sherry was being seen in her room, Harmony stayed by Ralph's side, offering him assistance when needed. It was the first time Ralph had seen Harmony since the wedding. He was grateful to her for standing by him at this time. Ralph had never noticed before that Harmony stood a few inches taller than Sherry and was a little slenderer.

Both sisters have long brown hair hanging to their shoulders, but

Harmony's was curly. Whether or not Harmony's hair curl was natural or not, he wasn't too sure, but it did give her a sexier look. Eyeing Harmony's body, when he thought she wasn't watching, Ralph could see the differences between the sisters. Harmony's figure was boyish, with slim hips and small breasts, whereas Sherry had large breasts and rounded hips.

While Sherry was in the hospital being examined by the doctors, Harmony stayed with Ralph in the waiting room. They talked as he paced. Harmony tried keeping him calm.

"You must be Ralph," the doctor said, coming up to him and shaking his hand.

"I am Sherry's Sister, Harmony," she said, breaking into the conversation.

"Hello Harmony. I know we have never met, but looking at you, I would say you look a lot like your sister," the doctor said.

Turning back to Ralph, he said, "Ralph, your wife is fine. We put her to bed, but I'm afraid the baby isn't due for a couple of days yet."

"Then shouldn't I take her home?"

"We would prefer it if you leave her here for observation," the doctor said, "We will call you the moment the time comes. Even though it is time for the baby's arrival, all she had at this time was a fault's labor."

"If you think it's the right thing to do, doctor."

"I do, go home, get some rest. You are going to need it."

"Okay, I will. But first, I want to see her."

"That will be fine. She is in room 302," the doctor told him.

"You won't forget to call me, will you?"

"No, I promise, you will be the first to be notified."

Harmony rode with him in the elevator without saying a word. Sherry was propped up in bed watching television when they walked in.

"Hey, you two," Sherry said, opening her arms for a hug, "Am I glad to see the two of you."

"How are you feeling, Sherry?" her sister asked.

"She's my girl, and I know she is feeling great," Ralph said, even though he wasn't too sure himself.

Ralph stayed by Sherry's bed for two hours, in which time he fell asleep three times.

"I think it's time for you to go home and get some sleep," Sherry told him. "I'll be fine with Harmony here with me."

"Are you sure?"

"Positive. Now go home."

Bending over the bed, Ralph kissed her passionately, then stood and walked out the door. For some reason, Harmony walked him to his car.

"I'll stop by later to see how you are doing."

"I'll be fine," he said, "She is just having a baby."

"She is having just a baby? That's playing it cool. Most men have a harder time than the women does," Harmony teased.

Laughing, he got in the car and drove home.

CHAPTER 28

Ralph drove back to their apartment in a daze. He was torn between staying with his wife and doing as the doctor suggested, to go home and get some needed rest. Knowing Harmony would be with Sherry, Ralph was able to relax a bit.

Knowing Harmony had volunteered to stay with her sister, so he could go home and get some rest, saved him from having to worry about a mishap. After Harmony walked him to his car, she went back inside.

Arriving home, Ralph tried watching television, but found he couldn't concentrate. Without Sherry in the house, the house felt empty. Nervous and lonely, Ralph decided to get ready for bed.

Stripping down, he threw his clothes in the hamper, then climbed into the shower. With the water as hot as he could stand it, he let the heat pour into his body. It had a relaxing effect and made him drowsy.

Out of the shower, Ralph sat on the edge of the bed. He was tired, but he missed Sherry. He needed to feel her soft, warm body lay next to him. Making sure the house was secure, he locked up and then pulled back the covers. Just as he was ready to crawl under the covers, the doorbell rang.

Who the hell could that be?

In the habit of sleeping in the nude, Ralph wrapped the damp towel around his waist. Wearily, he went to the door. Opening the door, he was surprised to see his sister-in-law standing there.

"Harmony, what are you doing?"

"I told you I would stop by. Can I come in?" she asked.

Stepping aside, he watched her enter.

"I thought you were staying with Sherry?"

"I was, but the doctor made me go home too."

In her arms were two boxes. Harmony was wearing a pink summer dress open at the neck, showing a little breast. Her feet were bare in soft sandals.

"Is Sherry all right?"

"As good as could be," she said, laughing.

"What's so funny?"

"You're funny. Before you were so sure, now you're not too sure, are you?"

"Not really."

"I didn't think so."

For some unexplained reason, Harmony was making him feel on the uncomfortable side. For a while, he thought about calling Vanessa to keep him company. Now, with Harmony here, it was too late.

"Why are you here?" he asked.

"I thought we both could use a little company and get to know each other better," she told him.

"Then, I'm glad you came," he said, smiling.

Not having any reason to suspect her real purpose, Ralph led her into the living room. As Harmony moved to sit on the couch, Ralph decided to put some clothes on.

"Excuse me a moment," he said.

Disappearing into his bedroom. When he came from the bedroom, he was wearing shorts and a T-shirt. Choosing a chair nearby, Ralph opened the boxes as they talked. The first box contained a bottle of gin, the other had two glasses.

"What are these for?"

"I thought we could have a couple of drinks to celebrate the birth of your son or daughter."

"That was thoughtful," Ralph said.

Taking the gifts to the bar, he mixed them both Tom Collins.

"Would you mind turning on the CD player?" Heather asked.

"Not at all, what would you like to hear?"

"Something soft and relaxing," Harmony said.

After placing the CDs in the player, he turned to go back to his seat. Instead, he found his sister-in-law wasn't sitting where he left her, but standing close to him. Nearly knocking her over when he turned, his reaction was to quickly grab her around the waist to keep her on her feet.

With her arms wide in an open invitation, Harmony knew he would catch her.

He stuttered, "What?"

He had a little surprised look on his face at seeing her so close.

"I thought we could dance a little. It might let you relax."

A smile broke out on his face. He could use a little comfort right now, he thought.

Taking his sister-in-law in his arms, they began to glide slowly and smoothly around the room. Harmony felt good in his arms. She felt a lot different from Sherry. He didn't remember Harmony dancing this close to him at the wedding reception. This wasn't Sherry, the sensation was so relaxing, Ralph let his thoughts pass by.

For some unknown reason, Ralph began comparing the sisters. Sherry, being shorter, always laid her head against his chest as they danced. Taller, Harmony was able to lay her head on his shoulder. Where Sherry was somewhat difficult to lead, Harmony was easy.

Having not had sex in a while, Ralph quickly became aware of her petite body and its subtle moves. Harmony hung on him like a cheap coat. Her small, hard breasts pressed against his chest. Her slim hips brushed against his. Not only did the woman feel good in his arms, but her movements had a way of charging his ardor.

After a couple of drinks too many, Harmony took the initiative. Being Ralph wasn't a drinker, he was feeling no pain. He couldn't remember how long they danced or how much booze they consumed. All he knew was, his resistance was gone, and he wanted her. The inevitable happened.

When the music stopped playing, they didn't move, yet held each other close. Ralph didn't want to let the other escape. Her arms were still draped around his shoulders. Her mouth was close to his ear as she whispered to him.

"I haven't felt this relaxed in ages."

Her voice seemed deep and erotic to him, stirring his senses. She seemed as turned on, sexually, as he was. Leaning into him, Ralph realized her lips were only inches from his. Temptation overruled his conscience. His intent was to kiss her softly, then walk away. But with the first touch of her lips and the feel of her slender body pressed willingly against his, Ralph's good intentions went for naught.

As Harmony's tongue invaded his mouth, their kisses deepened. With the situation totally out of control, Harmony ground her hips into his. Unable to stop himself, he returned her kiss harder than he had meant to. That was when Harmony knew she had him.

Momentarily breaking the kiss, she leaned back. As she leaned back, she was able to press her hips against his swollen erection. Feeling him, she slowly began grinding her hips against him.

"Oh, Ralph, it's been so long since I last made love. Make love to me here, now," she whispered, nibbling his ear.

This intensified his pleasure and robbed him of his senses. No longer thinking clearly, the combination of the booze and passion, he felt consumed with a raging desire. Letting his body rule his mind, his hands moved slowly and tenderly down her slender back to her waist, then to her soft, flat bottom. Grasping her soft cheeks in both hands, he pulled her hips roughly against him. Because it had been so long, his need only spurred him on.

CHAPTER 29

Her perfume had a different aroma from Sherry's, but it was just as intoxicating. Suddenly, he didn't care whether she was his wife's sister or not. It was evident Harmony didn't care either.

"How long has it been?" she whispered.

When he mumbled a response, she stuck her tongue in his ear.

Being honest, he mumbled, "About two months."

"You must be hungry," she said.

She continued rubbing against him to keep him stimulated. Harmony could feel him fighting her, but in the end, she knew she had won the battle.

"You'll never know how hungry I am," Ralph said.

"I will if you show me. Now, tonight," she told him.

Needing to hear nothing more, Ralph took her hand. Staring into her eyes, Ralph saw what he thought he wanted to see. Knowing she had won, Harmony didn't want to wait any longer. She led him down the hall to the bedroom, she used while staying with them.

She had wanted to use her sister's bed too, but he had nixed that. They quickly undressed, letting their eyes scan the other's body. She is a beauty, and she was very slender, almost streamlined. Sherry was softer and more solid, more athletic.

Harmony's thighs were thinner, and her hips more boyish. Her breasts were much smaller, not as beautiful. In her heated condition, he saw that her small red nipples were puckered with passion.

Harmony knew Ralph was lost to her spell. Taking his hand, she pulled him with her to the bed. Naked, Harmony liked what she saw and envied her sister. His erection seemed bigger than any of the men she had ever been with. She knew this was going to be good.

Landing on her, Ralph was amazed at how silky her body felt beneath him. Quickly, without preliminaries, she wrapped her long legs around his back. Wet with anticipation, Harmony took him easily.

Finished, they lay exhausted, still locked together. Both were tired and were breathing heavily from their frenzied lovemaking. Harmony had never had sex like this before. It was very hot, and very intense, yet soft and yielding. She needed and wanted more of him.

Somewhere in the distance, Ralph heard the telephone ringing. At that moment, reality came charging back. Rolling to his feet, Ralph sprang to the telephone. It was the hospital calling. Something inside him snapped. Sick at heart, Ralph couldn't comprehend what he was being told.

What had he done to his wife? Guilt ate at him. Sherry is in the hospital having his baby, and all he could do was to have meaningless sex with her sister.

Realizing something else, Ralph found that what he had just done was just a release for him. It meant nothing more to him than a stupid mistake. To make matters worse, the sex wasn't even as good as it was with Sherry. Why did he do it?

"Oh my God, what have I done?" he said aloud.

"Settle down," Harmony said, "What we have just done countless of others have done before us. We are not the only people in the world to steal some forbidden love. As for me, I loved it."

"But she's your sister," he screamed at her, "Don't you have any feelings?"

"She's your wife," Harmony said without guilt, "Besides, she had it coming."

Guilt gnawed at him. Not wanting to hear anything more or to be near her any longer, Ralph hurriedly dressed.

As he ran from the room, he shouted, "What kind of a woman are you?"

"A woman who gets what she wants."

"No matter whom it hurts?"

At the end of the hall, all he heard her say was, "You know it, baby."

At the staircase, he all but fell down the stairs, stumbling as he went. In the foyer, he bumped into the table near the front door. Seeing his car keys, as they dropped to the floor, Ralph grabbed for them. Scooping up the keys, Ralph made it through the door, leaving it wide open in his wake.

Quickly sliding into the front seat of his old car, he slammed the door shut. Sick with grief, he numbly sat behind the wheel, staring out the window. Sweat poured from his body. His eyes burned from the salt.

Having trouble finding where to put the key, he began to cry. Finally getting the key in place, Ralph turned the key. In that same instant, he tromped on the accelerator. The engine roared. With his foot on the gas and tears stinging his eyes, the vehicle careened across the yard, sending gravel flying in all directions.

Loud popping noises sounded, as the gravel sprayed across the yard, striking Harmony's car. As Ralph's car shot out of the driveway, he nearly struck an oncoming car. Tires squealed and horns blared as the other car swerved to avoid hitting him.

Pain and confusion shot through him. Getting away was all he had on his mind. From the horrible aftermath of what he had done, he washed everything from his mind. All thoughts of his sister, wife, and baby-to-be were forgotten.

Knowing he could not go back to his wife until he told her the whole truth, Ralph drove wildly away from town. Wild thoughts kept filling his head. It seemed impossible to clear his mind. Back and forth, his thoughts bounced like a ball between Sherry and Harmony.

Realization hit him. Harmony never asked where he was going. All he could hear, in his head, as he ran from the room, was her high-pitched laughter. What a fool he had been, fooling around with his wife's sister.

Harmony is nothing but a tramp, and he fell for it. All Harmony wanted was to hurt Sherry. Now he has hurt her too. What did Sherry do to Harmony to make her sister want to hurt her as she did? Didn't she realize what she was doing to her mother and father?

Suddenly, out of the corner of his eye, a familiar road appeared in front of him. Quickly turning the wheel, he felt the car skid, then swerve. Careening around the corner, Ralph straightened out on the road he wanted.

Picking up speed, he met each winding and twisting curve as he sped through the canyon with casual ease. Knowing he was going much too fast for the existing conditions, he tried to slow down, but his mind wouldn't let him. Torment overrode good intentions.

Going too fast for the corner he had to take, his car struck the guard rails next to the river. Not caring or thinking straight, he did only what his brain was telling him to. Self-loathing kept his foot tight on the gas pedal.

Before he realized it, another deadly hairpin curve midway through the canyon came upon him. This time, without any hesitation, his car broke through the guardrail. The only sounds were those of metal tearing and an engine roaring, as the car flew out over the raging river. Headlights shone briefly on the walls of the canyon, just before the car plunged nose-first into the river. In seconds, the car sank from sight, taking its passenger with it.

Sounds of squealing tires, rending metal, and a screaming engine lasted all of thirty seconds. Now, one minute later, the canyon that had been filled with odd sorts of sounds and lights was again quiet and dark.

CHAPTER 30

Back at the house, Harmony remained in bed, thinking Ralph would be back. Deep satisfaction spread through her body. Lying with her hands behind her head and a big smile on her face, Harmony waited for Ralph to return. Her thoughts were, once Ralph cools down, he will return to me. He will see that having an affair with his sister-in-law wasn't going to hurt anything. If anything, it will give him a diversion from everyday sex with just one woman.

Much later, after listening to the phone ring a dozen times, it was evident Ralph was not returning. Angrily, Harmony slid from the bed. Reminisce of his sperm flowed down her leg. In a fury, she dressed and left. Downstairs, Harmony found the front door wide open, as Ralph had left it. Grabbing her keys from the floor, lying near the overturned table, Harmony left as Ralph did, not closing the door behind her.

Sexually satisfied, Harmony smiled to herself as she climbed into her car. She could still feel him moving deep inside her. What she remembered most was the moment he deposited his seed deep inside her. With the sweet memory of what happened, she drove away, not looking back.

As Harmony drove toward her apartment, she began thinking about what had just transpired. Quickly, the smile faded from her face. Thinking of what she had done finally hit her. How was she going to explain this to her sister or to her mother and father, for that matter?

Suddenly, she was heart-sick with despair. Thoughts of the good sex she just had with Ralph kept swimming through her mind. The sex was great for her, but now her family was going to suffer because of her hatred.

Sherry had been a lucky girl. Now, because of the hated she had in her head, Sherry's marriage will be over. It was what Harmony had hoped for. The only difference was, Harmony had hoped to steal Ralph for herself. She was younger and thought of herself as prettier.

Now that Harmony had accomplished what she wanted, she felt differently. Guilt feelings washed into her soul. Her guilt made her vulnerable for the first time in years. Harmony had taken the one thing Sherry wanted and broken it, but in the process, she had beaten herself, too.

Yes, she had beaten her sister by bedding her husband. Now, Harmony realized too late what she had done made her lose more than her sister. She lost her job, her sister and possibly her mother and father's love.

Harmony had lost everything because the stupid bastard did not want her. The self-righteous prick hated her, instead of loving her as she had imagined. It was the whole rotten story of her life. Every guy she ever had sexually, left her after the first or second time.

What is it that she does that makes men leave her so quickly? Mostly, they left her for other women. What hurt the most was the man telling her she didn't know how to fuck. Well, fuck the world, she was getting off.

Once Sherry finds out what she has done, her sister will have no choice but to ostracize her from the business. Her parents will be torn too. Before Harmony knew what she was doing, she was miles from town. With a heavy heart, she kept driving. No longer caring where she was going, she drove all night, stopping only once or twice for gas and food.

The next morning, unable to hold her eyes open any longer, she stopped at the first motel she came to.

Back home on a Gurney, writhing with pain, Sherry screamed as she was being wheeled to the operating room, "Where is my husband?"

Sherry knew it wouldn't be long now before the baby was born. Her labor pains were coming very quickly. Now was the time she needed Ralph with her. Where was he?

"I don't know," the nurse told her.

As the nurse began prepping Sherry, the nurse said, "We did call to tell him you would be delivering soon."

"It shouldn't take him this long to get here," Sherry moaned.

"Relax, Mrs. Anderson. He probably got caught in traffic."

Suddenly, another great shot of pain racked through her body. Pain so intense, Sherry began rolling her head on the pillow. Sweat covered her body and face, blinding her.

"Maybe he had car trouble," The nurse said.

Trying to help Sherry relax, she bathed Sherry's face with a cold, wet face cloth. When it was time for the baby to arrive, an orderly quickly wheeled her Gurney into the delivery room. Prepped for delivery, the doctors waited as long as they could for Ralph to arrive. Ralph never got to the hospital for the birth of his son.

Chapter 31

Morning sunlight shone on a large two-story mansion sitting high on a hill overlooking the river. In her bedroom, Candy Farrell was just sliding out of bed. She went to the window to see what her two Poodles were barking at. They had awakened her with their incessant barking.

Glancing at the clock, she saw it was only seven o'clock. What could those dogs be barking at so early in the morning? Not seeing what they were barking at from the window, she went downstairs, where she could look out the sliding glass door.

Peering out of the large sliding glass door, leading to an outside patio, she still didn't see anything. In the distance, she could see her two apricot color poodles, by the edge of her property, barking at something on the other side of the fence.

Something upriver she couldn't see from the patio was upsetting her girls. It was unusual for them to make so much noise, especially at this time of morning. I guess I'll have to go investigate, Candy told herself.

After quickly changing into some warmer clothing, she rushed down the stairs to quiet her dogs. Slipping on a light summer jacket to fend off the icy dew, Candy went out the back door to the edge of the hill leading down toward the river.

"What is it, girls? What do you see?"

Her highly agitated poodles kept barking.

"What is it? Is someone there?" Candy asked again.

Carefully, she made her way through the cool, damp grass to the bottom of the hill, near the edge of the river. By the time she got there, her feet felt damp inside her canvas sneakers. Whatever the dogs were barking had to be much further up the river, she thought.

Scanning the immediate area, she still couldn't see anything.

Trained not to leave the yard, unless they were with their master, the dogs stayed at the edge of the property barking until she told them to follow. Deciding to risk the walk, Candy slowly walked up the riverbank with the dogs heeling. Further on, after stepping onto a ready-made path leading upriver toward the canyon, Candy gave her dogs their lead.

The dogs came to a sudden halt thirty yards away and stopped barking. Curious, yet leery, Candy stepped to higher ground for a better view. What lay ahead? Even her dogs wouldn't approach further. Something had to be laying half out of the water. At first, Candy hesitated. Then, swallowing her fear moved closer.

Upon closer inspection, Candy realized what she was seeing was a man. The body was lying motionless up to his waist in the water. Her first thought was, he couldn't possibly be alive. Yet, to be sure of the condition the man was in, Candy moved closer. Bending over the body, she first checked for a pulse. There was a pulse, but a very weak pulse. On further examination, she found the man was badly hurt.

Gazing up the river from where the body had come from, she couldn't imagine how the young man had gotten in such bad condition. Not only was his face lacerated his chest and arms were also. From the way his extremities lay, she knew there were multiple brakes.

Struggling, Candy pulled the body from the water onto the bank. She knew she could be doing further damage, but in her opinion, he would surely die if he remained in the water much longer.

Feeling the man was as safe as he could be for now, Candy hurried back to her home. Seeing her the two male servants setting the table on the back terrace for her morning breakfast, she hollered.

"Peter, Harry, please come quickly."

Dropping what they had been doing, they rushed to Candy's side.

"What is it, ma'am?" Peter asked.

"There is a man lying in the river upstream. He's too big and hurt for me to carry alone. Get the lounge chair from the patio, Harry," she said, pointing at the younger of the two men.

"Peter, you come with me."

As Harry retrieved the lounge, Peter followed his employer down the hill to the river to help with the man. When Harry got there, the two men placed the body carefully on the lounge.

"Put him in my bed," Candy told them. "It will be easier for me to take care of him there."

The footing along the riverbank was treacherous, especially when carrying a heavy load, but they made it without mishap. After getting the man into the bed, Candy had the servants help undress him. Undressed and clean, it was easier for Candy to see how badly slashed and broken he was.

How did this man survive? He could have bled to death or drowned. He had to have been in the water a long time. From the looks of his skin, she would say hours. To see just how much damage the man suffered, Candy began an extensive examination.

At thirty-eight years of age, Candy had been a promising surgeon. Her specialty was skin grafting. That had been six years ago. Her career as a doctor ended the day she lost her husband under her own knife.

Other surgeons had told her not to do the operation, but she wouldn't listen. Going ahead with the surgery as scheduled, he died. It was a conflict of interest, she was told. She was in no shape to perform such a delicate task.

Since that day, she had never set foot in any hospital again. Although Candy kept up with medical changes and other important data, she wasn't sure of herself.

Now, at the age of forty-four, a man whose life was in the balance lay before her. Her skill could keep him alive. She could prove she was still a great surgeon and make this man handsome again.

Not only was the man's body broken his arms and legs, plus his face was badly lacerated. Gently touching his face, Candy could tell his cheekbones were crushed and his jaw cruelly broken. Both eyes were detached from their original settings and were bleeding. Having no idea what the man looked like before, she pondered the idea of fixing him herself, here in her home.

Then she thought, should she report him to the police? If she did and someone wanted him dead, then she would also be a target. By not reporting him, no one needs to know if he was dead or alive. If he couldn't remember who he is or how he became injured, no one would ever know.

All these thoughts and more were running through her mind. Not only did they frighten her, but they were also making her leery. Making a quick decision, she decided to do the surgery and hope everything turned out for the best.

Her bedroom was huge with a lot of floor space. The room ran the entire length of the house in the rear. Both sides of the room had huge windows that faced both east and west. To the rear was a double patio door leading out to a wooden deck, twelve feet above the lower patio. Built into the deck, just outside her bedroom door, was a six-man hot tub. The view from the hot tub overlooking the river and surrounding mountains was spectacular.

During the summer months, low-flying clouds would cover the tips of the mountains straight ahead. Winter months, those same mountain tops would be covered with snow. Below the mountain and at the end of her property, flowed a wide swift swift-running river. Trees blocked her view of the ocean, except during the winter when the trees were bare.

Because the size of her bedroom was so large, Candy had her servants bring all her medical equipment to her room, where she set up the clinic. She was again hoping to perform a miracle. It would be a miracle needed to save the life of this man. Knowing she had to make a difficult decision, Candy began pacing. Pacing always helped her thought process.

From time to time, she would stop her pacing to look at him. Finally deciding on what she must do, she quickly overcame her fear of the past. To keep him alive, she had no other choice but to operate.

After six hours of tedious work on his body alone, she stopped long enough for a bite to eat. With his body in a cast, the man looked like a mummy. Now, someday, once his limbs completely healed, this man should have the use of his arms and legs again. His face was another story. Candy knew she would have to operate again.

Six weeks later, Candy removed the casts, and his therapy began. Working his limbs became a daily chore. At night, she sat by his bed to keep an eye on him. Sitting by the bed night after night, she never gave up hope that he would survive and one day wake up.

During that time, whenever she would fall asleep at his bedside, one of the servants would watch him. For her comfort and stability, her servants placed a small bed in the room near where her patient slept. She wanted to remain in the same room, near her patient at all times, because her time was his if and when he would need her.

After a few hours of rest, with very little sleep, the servants would wake her at her request. At that time, she would freshen up by showering, changing clothes and eating.

CHAPTER 32

Early one morning, as the sun began its rise over the trees, Candy lay in a twilight zone. Halfway between awake and asleep, she was still able to hear birds singing. Opening her eyes, she listened to the sounds. This would be a wonderful time for a miracle, she thought.

Rising, she looked at him. The casts still covered his body. The only difference his eyes were open. It happened. A miracle actually happened. At least in Candy's eyes, his eyes opening was a miracle. Looking deeper into her patient's eyes, she saw something she had been dreading. Dull eyes stared up at her. They had lost their shine. He was blind.

"Are you awake?" She asked softly.

"Yes." He mumbled softly.

His voice was very hoarse, almost inaudible.

"What is your name?"

Laying in silence for a few moments, he finally answered, "I can't remember."

"What can you remember?"

Again, there was a long silence.

"Nothing," he croaked.

"You were in terrible shape when I found you. All I did this time was repair your broken bones. I didn't want to do plastic surgery until I spoke to you first."

"What do I look like?" he asked.

"Physically, you were not very pretty. Both your legs and arms were broken. I'm surprised you weren't dead."

"I can't remember who I am, let alone what I use to look like?" he murmured.

"Since you don't know who you are, or what you looked like before, would you agree to let me fix the situation?"

"What would you have to do?"

"I'd have to do Plastic surgery. I am a licensed plastic surgeon."

"How badly do I look?"

"You were not a pretty sight."

"What have you already done?"

"I mended both your arms and legs, which were broken. Your jaw and cheekbones were crushed, which will have to be reconstructed. I'm sorry to say, I think your eyesight will be lost forever. If I had not repaired as much as I did, you would not be able to speak."

Unable to concentrate or retain what he was being told, he kept repeating his questions.

"What do you have left to do?"

"To enable me to make your looks more appealing, it's detrimental I operate again and soon. I cannot offer any guarantees, except that I will try and hope you will allow me the chance to correct your looks for the better. There will be no charge. I will be doing this for both you and me."

"Will you be giving me my same face?"

"Since I don't know what you used to look like, I won't be able to do that."

"Didn't I have a picture on me?"

"You had nothing in your clothes, only you're broken body. We searched for clues to find out where you came from, but we could learn nothing. Nothing was in any of the newspapers about an accident. We bought newspapers from fifty miles around."

"When do you want to operate?"

"I'll operate as soon as possible, if you agree."

"Since I don't know what I looked like before, do you have an idea how I will look like when you're finished?"

"How would you like to look?"

"Handsome."

"Handsome, you will be."

"Do it."

"Good. Now, once you're ready, we will begin therapy."

"What kind of therapy?"

"Since you will not have your sight anymore, you will have to learn to know everything by touch and smell."

Early the next morning, Candy started her project. This man was going to be her special creation. The operation would be extensive and costly, but she had the expertise and the funds to do it.

As she started her preparation, Candy felt the old thrill return. Letting her skill take over, she began to operate as if there was never been a lapse in time. Several operations would be needed to complete the job. All the operations and healing time combined will take two to three years to complete.

CHAPTER 33

When Sherry came home from the hospital, she couldn't believe Ralph never came to visit. What had happened to Ralph? No one, not even Vanessa, knew where Ralph had gone.

Vanessa helped Sherry when she first got home from the hospital. Learning Harmony was also missing, and Sherry began to believe Ralph ran away with Harmony.

"Could the two of them run off together?"

"No way, Sherry, Ralph loves you and doesn't care much for your sister."

"Then, why are they both gone?"

As time went by, Sherry was sure her husband and her sister had run off together. Her parents were beside themselves. When Sherry went back to work at the clinic, Vanessa was available to watch her nephew.

The baby took his first steps within the first year. Now, at two, Gerald was beginning to talk. Because Gerald's father has been missing for the last two years, Sherry decided to give Gerald her maiden name of Sergeant. Sherry was very bitter. She had immense hatred for both her sister and her husband.

"Vanessa, if you ever hear from your brother, tell him for me that I don't ever want to see or talk to him again."

"He might have a good explanation, Sherry."

"Like he had an accident and lost his memory?"

"Could be?"

"I don't buy it. As far as I'm concerned, all men are the same."

As time moved on, so did her hatred. It would have been better had she had known the plight of the two. Even after all this time, Sherry still had a sinking feeling that Ralph ran off with Harmony. Hurt and anger ruled her life. Her bitterness made it impossible for her to be around other people, especially men.

To satisfy her own curiosity, Sherry hired a private investigator to find them. For a while, she heard from him at least once a week. A while later, it was twice a month. Then she stopped hearing from him at all. After three years, and thousands of dollars, she still had no word from either of them, or where they were.

Candy's only comfort came from her son, her parents, and Vanessa. Just having them made her feel lucky.

Vanessa, now twenty-seven, was hurt most by what she thought was her brother's betrayal. At first, she was angry with him. Then, when the police found Ralph's car, upside down in the river. Now, the possibility of Ralph being dead was gone. A deep dread and longing settled in.

Divers found the car upside down in the deepest part of the river. Notifying the police, a crane and wreckers were brought to the scene. Divers attached the rigs to the car and pulled it out. No one was inside the car.

Checking the car, the police found traces of clothing and skin on some of the scraped metal. Since the car had only been in the water a couple of months, it would be almost impossible to identify whose the cloth and skin belonged to. According to the police, they think the driver was thrown from the vehicle and drowned.

Because of the current of the river, they assumed the driver was most likely swept out to sea. Sherry and Vanessa were not too sure. Ralph could have drowned and been swept away, as the police think, or maybe Ralph purposely crashed the car into the river to keep anyone from looking for him.

Both girls went with the last scenario. Finding Harmony, they would most likely find Ralph. If Ralph weren't with her, then they might believe what the police think.

Wait, was all they could do now.

Chapter 34

Miles away, down the river, a man sits in a wheelchair, overlooking the river. The feel of the sun on his face felt wonderful. It had been a long time since his face was bared to the sun. Now with the bandages gone, he felt wonderful. Even though he couldn't see, the river the sounds and smells of the river were enjoyable to him.

Since he couldn't see anything, the tools he had to learn would be touch, hearing and smell. Learning those skills was not going to be easy. Yesterday, he had gotten rid of the bandages that covered his face. Today, he was to start intensive therapy. The process of making him mentally aware was about to begin.

For days after the operations, the man tried to think of something, anything to tell him about his past. If he could just remember, maybe, just maybe, she could find out who he used to be.

For some reason, he did not feel like the person in this skin. Maybe it was because of an accident, he forgot everything. Then again, maybe it wasn't. What could have been so bad for him to push whatever it was so far back in his mind, to make him forget? Maybe some day his memory would return, or maybe someone in his past will recognize him.

To be realistic, he knew that was impossible. He was not the same person he was before. A man with a new face would not be recognizable to anyone in his past. If he could not even remember what his real face looked like, how would anyone else know? Tears began rolling down his cheeks.

Feeling someone's presence, he tensed.

"How are we this morning?" she asked.

"I'm fine, and how are you?"

For the first time, he realized, he did not know her name.

"How long have I been here?" the man asked.

"You have been here about one year now, why?"

"I just realized I don't know your name."

Laughing, she said. "Call me Candy. Since we don't know your name, I'll name you Sheldon after my grandfather."

"I would like that."

"Good, Sheldon will be your name."

"What is my last name going to be?"

"Stevens, I'll call you Sheldon Stevens."

"You have a nice voice," he told her, "I can imagine why your parents named you Candy."

"Well, thank you. That is a nice thing to say."

"I would like to know more about you, Candy," he said.

"In due time," Candy said.

"Right now, we start your therapy."

"What do I have to do?"

"I realize it has been a year now, so therapy will be a little hard on you."

"What kind of therapy? Don't I have use of my arms and legs?"

"Merely having to use of your limbs is only part of the picture. You also must know how to use them to help you with your blindness."

"What do I do?"

"Sit here at this table," she told him.

"You'll have to help me."

"I'll help you only for a short while. Starting this time, you must start counting your steps, plus remember where everything is."

"What if someone moves something?"

"Nothing around this house should be moved. If you are somewhere else besides here, that will be different. If you are away from familiar surroundings, as you are now, just take the arm of the person you are with. Let them lead you. Don't forget, you always have to remember where you are and how many steps it takes to get where you're going."

Slowly, he stood. Feeling wobbly, as he stood, he felt like he needed to grab something, to hold him up. Feeling the chair. He had been sitting in a chair rubbing the back of his legs helped him a little.

It was a weird feeling standing alone, without help. Not knowing Candy was nearby, he was very unsure of himself. Summoning some nerve, even though he was afraid to move, he took a deep breath, then made himself move.

At first, unsure of where to step, he felt very clumsy. Suddenly, he got a whiff of perfume. Now knowing Candy was nearby, ready to help him, he wasn't satisfied with his feelings. Never having to help before, he felt vulnerable moving to another chair fifteen steps away.

Reaching the chair, he sat. Taking a deep breath to let the tension slide away, he felt shaky. Never needing help before, he knew he now had to learn to fend for himself. He also knew he now had to rely on others and learn to trust.

Feeling around him, he realized he was now on the other side of a round table.

"This is a round table," he said.

"Very good," she said, "Now what is it made of?"

Feeling it again, he concentrated his efforts. Quickly pulling his hands away from the table, he realized that one side was hotter than the other.

"Are we in the sun now?"

"What do you mean now?"

"Well, it feels hotter in this chair, where it wasn't as hot in the other."

"Very good," she said again, "These are the things you have to be aware of and a lot more."

"I'm trying," he said, "Oh, by the way, I am sitting at a glass table. Correct?"

"Yes, you are sitting at a glass table. You will do better in days to come. Now, tell me what is in front of you."

Not knowing how far away the object was, he slowly moved his hand one way, then the other, until he touched an object. Feeling it, he began to fondle it.

"It's a bowl," he said, sitting back in the chair.

"Keep going."

Reaching again, he let his hands move over the rim of the bowl. Picking up the first object he touched, it felt sort of round. Unable to see it, he squeezed it. It was hard. Rubbing the object with his hands, he hit something that seemed to be coming out of it. After smelling it, he took a small bite.

"It's an apple."

"Are you sure?"

Sniffing where he had bitten into it, there wasn't much of a smell. Taking a larger bite, he savored it, but didn't swallow. Instead, he spat it into his hand.

"It tastes like an apple," he said proudly.

"That was good, but what if what you bit into was poison?"

"How would I know that?"

"All you have is to touch and smell. If you can't tell from either of those practices, ask someone. If there is no one around and it doesn't smell, break it or cut it open, then smell it. Never bite into anything or eat something until you are sure of what it is."

"This isn't going to be easy, is it?"

"No one said it was going to be easy, and it's going to get more difficult as we learn."

CHAPTER 35

Two thousand miles away, in another state, another mother was playing with her thirteen-month-old daughter.

She looked identical to her father, Harmony thought. Oh, how I miss her father. If only I had done things differently that night. Maybe everything would be different now.

In the last two years, Harmony constantly thought of the family she left behind. Would they ever forgive her, knowing what she had done? Maybe she should ask for their forgiveness, after all, they are her family. She still remembers clearly the events that took place that night. She can't have Ralph, but she will always have the memories and this one cute little reminder.

The night Harmony ran, she stayed on the road for two weeks. Trying to find a place where she could get lost wasn't easy. Of all the places to pick, she picked a place where there were a lot of men. It was a construction town, and construction was booming. Besides, there were a lot of men, and she loved sex.

A few months later, Harmony realized she was pregnant. Now, she would have more than memories of that night, unless the baby wasn't Ralph's. If the baby is Ralph's, maybe she should go back home, just to show off the baby. Maybe Ralph will relent and take me in because of the baby.

As the days wore on, Harmony began thinking deeper on the subject. It was the first time in her life, she ever thought of anything seriously. Moving from the small town to the city, Harmony found a small, cheap apartment with two bedrooms. The baby would now have its own room.

Harmony had wiped out her savings buying things for the baby. What hurt most was the day she had to go to the hospital for the delivery. There wasn't anyone there for her. There was no man to hold her, no man to say how happy he was, and there wasn't any family to support her.

Regret filled her. Sadly, Harmony didn't know how to make everything right again. After the baby was born, Harmony found a low-paying job just to make ends meet. It wasn't as a doctor, but it was work. She named her daughter Rebecca.

Harmony missed her nights out. She didn't have the time or the money to go out and enjoy the fast life. Having a child to take care of gave her more responsibility. No one but Harmony heard the baby's first words or watched Rebecca take her first steps. For the first time in her life, Harmony felt truly alone. Sadly, she had no one to blame but herself.

Now, after two years away from home, Harmony contemplated a move back home. Should she tell everyone the truth about the detective? Become clean with everyone?

The detective Sherry hired to find her did find her. Actually, the detective found her in the hospital, getting ready to deliver. Being a desperate woman, Harmony reverted to her old self. Forget about coming clean.

I'll show my sister, Harmony thought. Using her womanly wiles, Harmony propositioned the detective into not telling anyone where she was.

The day Harmony first met the detective was in the hospital. She opened her eyes only to look into the eyes of a tired, old, obese man staring at her. At first, she thought the man was in the wrong room. Then he spoke.

"Good morning, Harmony Sergeant," the man said.

"Who are you?" she replied.

"Let's just say your sister has been looking for you."

"A detective. Now that you found me, are you going to tell her where I am?"

"That depends."

"On what?"

"How badly do you want not to be found?"

"What is my sister paying you?"

"Enough," he said.

"What would it take, beside money, for you to keep your mouth shut?"

"How about a month in your bed?" he told her.

Even though Harmony felt repulsed by his physical being, she knew she had to give him what he wanted, or he would tell. Closing her eyes, Harmony wondered if she could go through with such a deal with this man.

"A relationship with me will give you time to get on your feet and give me some enjoyment," the man added quickly.

"I will be getting out of the hospital tomorrow," Harmony told him.

She was willing to stay hidden even though the thought of this piece of slime touching her, let alone having sex with her, turned her stomach.

"If you still want to pick me up, with Rebecca, you can have your wish."

After Harmony said the words, she wanted to puke. As she watched his immense body wobble from the room, she almost did. How could she sink so low as to let that slob touch her?

The next morning, the detective was waiting for her. He was sitting in her room as he waited for her to be released. Harmony carried

Rebecca to the car, while the man carried what she had for baggage.

The beat-up rust bucket he drove had a bad engine. The leather seats were worn and torn, and the car smelled of who knows what. Ten minutes later, the detective pulled into a seedy apartment building in the bad part of town. No sooner had they entered the apartment than he began to paw her.

"Put the baby in her crib," the man said.

"You have a crib for her?"

"I bought it last night."

"Is it clean?"

"Do you think I would let a child sleep where there were germs?"

"Seeing how you live, I wonder."

"I might be poor, but I am clean."

She had to admit that much about him. The small kitchen and the floors were clean. As she looked around the apartment, he began to undress.

"Come on, Harmony, daddy is waiting."

"Can't you wait until tonight?"

"It's been too long already," he told her.

Knowing she wouldn't be able to hold him off with words, Harmony began to undress. Normally, she would have told him off and left, but that would have only made matters worse. He could let her go, then turn around and tell Sherry where she was.

The fat man actually beat Harmony while getting undressed. Naked, she was repulsed by the sight of him. His belly hung down in several folds, hiding his small penis. She wondered how he found it to take a pee.

Undressed, Harmony got into the bed. Closing her eyes, she waited for him to take her. As his immense body moved onto the bed, his weight made the bed sag. To her surprise, as hard and horny as he seemed, he wanted more from her.

"Just do it," she said dryly.

"Not just yet. I can't wait to have you," he said, "but first I want what most men get, before having sex. Some old-fashioned necking."

Closing her eyes, Harmony opened her arms to him. She was happy he laid on his side, instead of upon her. Harmony to let him pull her close. The feel of his fat belly pressing against her almost made her sick. His fat, greasy lips found hers. His kiss was actually gentle as he tried to get her to enjoy what was to come. Most of the time, a man wouldn't have to work hard to get her in the mood. With this man, nothing worked.

Finally, as he moved over her, she opened her body for him. Feeling his immense belly press down on her made it difficult for her to breathe.

"Help me," he groaned.

Sliding an arm between them was difficult. Feeling all the fat slide on her arm disgusted her, but she managed. Once she had him inside her, it seemed to take him forever to achieve a climax. If it weren't for his immense size, he would probably be a good lover.

During the five months they lived together, the detective wrote to Sherry, telling her he still couldn't find her. His sexual desire never waned. He wanted her constantly, and she complied.

"Hey Harmony, come to bed, I need some loving."

"You always want loving. Don't you ever get enough?"

"Not with a woman like you."

As she moved into the bedroom, she saw his naked body. He seemed fatter than ever, and he always had a sweaty stink to him. At night, his stink turned her stomach. When she was on the bottom, how he liked it; his extended belly made it difficult for her to receive him.

Once Harmony talked him into letting her ride him, she found sex with him was much better. She didn't have to contend with his weight. With her on top. She found he had a quick trigger. At least she didn't have as long to suffer.

As the months wore on, Harmony began to wonder if this charade would ever end. One night, when they were in the missionary position, with him on top, pumping away, Harmony kept her eyes closed, trying to endure his pleasure. Suddenly, she felt him go rigid, as he did when he climaxed. With a mighty grunt, his full weight bore down on her.

"Hey man, get the fuck off of me, I can't breathe."

He never spoke or moved. Harmony tried pushing him from her, but she couldn't budge him. He was dead weight. Frightened, she began to scream. She screamed until her throat was sore. Finally, someone knocked on the door.

CHAPTER 36

"Is everything all right in there?" a voice shouted.

"No. Please help me," she shouted

The doorknob rattled, but the door didn't open.

"The door is locked," the voice said.

"Break it down," she cried.

With a splintering of wood, the door banged into the wall behind. A huge black man, around sixty years of age, strode into the room.

"Good Lord, girl. What do we have here?"

"I think he is dead," Harmony cried, "Can you please get him off me?"

"Is he your husband?"

"No. He is just an acquaintance."

"Are you a whore?"

"No."

"Then what you doing with a man like him, in you?"

"I owed him. Now, will you please help me?"

"If I do, you will owe me too."

"I don't care. Just get him off."

In seconds, the black man had pulled the slob from her. The man then carried him into the bathroom, only to deposit him into the tub. When the man came back, Harmony was sitting on the bed, almost naked. She had started to get dressed. The man stopped and stared at her. His throat went dry.

"Let's make sure you don't leave anything in this room the police can identify you with."

"The only thing that belongs to me is the baby in the other room."

"Is it the man's baby?"

"No."

"We have time," he said.

Harmony knew what he meant. Having just put on her panties and bra, Harmony, not wanting to be hurt by the black man, took them off.

"Lord, you look good."

Having never been with a black man before, Harmony nearly choked. Seeing his huge erection, for the first time, made her wonder. God, how in the hell was she going to take him. Knowing there was no use in fighting the situation, she lay back and raised her arms to him. His color was nearly purple, and the head of his erection was coal black.

Being, Harmony had just had sex with that fat slob who died, she knew she was well lubricated. To be truthful, liking sex as Harmony does, she was beginning to get excited, even though it was with the fat slob. Now, because the fat bastard hadn't come, she was about to let this bull have her. She hoped this black man, built the way he was, would ease her emotions.

"First things first," he said.

Waving his immense erection, he looked at her.

"Suck it."

For as much sex as Harmony has had, she has never done what this black man wanted her to do. Now, here was this huge black monster throbbing before her eyes. Kneeling, she touched it with her tongue, then, slowly opening her lips, she took him into her mouth. It wasn't long before he pushed her away.

"Get on your knees, on the bed, with your back toward me," he told her. She did as he asked. Feeling his erection touch her, then slide inside, she nearly fainted. He pounded her for a while, then put her on her back. Seeing the contrast of his color entering her white boy heightened her need. She screamed her climax, as he groaned his release inside her.

Out of breath and exhausted, they remained locked together. Ten minutes later, they disconnected and dressed.

"I have never had a white woman before."

"That makes us even. I've never been with a black man before."

"We have to get out of here," he said, "Let's get the baby and go."

"Where are we going?"

"We going to my place."

Carrying Rebecca, Harmony followed the black man to his car. It was a beat-up old Oldsmobile.

"Don't you live here?"

"No way, I was just visiting a friend when I heard your noise."

Harmony looked at her surroundings as she got in the man's car. From the looks of the car, the black man had to be poor. The interior was dirty, and the seats and upholstery were torn. When he started the engine, she thought the car was going to explode.

"How long do expect me to stay with you?" she asked, huddling against the door, with her daughter in her arms.

"How long can you stay?"

It wasn't much later before she could answer him. Pulling into a dirt space, near some tumbled down shacks, she saw the faces of other black men and women milling around with seemingly nothing to do. They looked lazy, shiftless and dirt-poor.

When she got out of the car, the other blacks stopped what they were doing to gawk at her. It was as if they had never seen a white woman before.

"Come on," he said

He led her down a short, dirty alley, where one shack stood alone. The shack had two rooms, and it was filthy. Dirty clothes and dishes littered the floors and the counters. She wanted to leave, but knew she wouldn't get too far. The only furniture was a worn couch, a black and white television, and a hot plate on a table in the corner. Two lamps were sitting on crates that he used for tables. Looking around in disgust, Harmony wondered what the man did for a living. He couldn't make much money.

"Where do you sleep?"

"The couch pulls out. Are you hungry?"

"Yes, but where is my baby going to sleep?"

Ignoring her, he continued to talk.

"Don't have much money," he said, "Would you like some pizza?"

"Pizza sounds good. Let me buy?"

"How long will you still stay?"

"Maybe for a week or two," Harmony said, "I have a lot of brain searching to do."

"What is your problem?"

"My family is my problem."

They ate pizza and drank warm beer. As soon as it got dark, he pulled out the hide-a-bed and turned on a small lamp nearby. For the baby, he pulled the two shabby chairs together. The arms of the chair would hold the baby inside.

Sitting, the man watched as Harmony got the baby ready for bed. Once the baby was settled, he spoke.

"You sure a beautiful woman," she told her.

As before, he watched her take off her clothes. He would never tire of seeing this white woman naked. Built like a boy, she had tiny breasts, slim hips and skinny legs. She was nothing like the big black women he had sex with.

He waited until she got on the bed before he undressed. Again, she felt the bed sag as he kneeled between her thighs. Harmony was impressed with his size. As he thrust inside her, Harmony realized she didn't even know his name. She couldn't remember the name of that fat slob she slept with.

Not knowing who this man is will be better, she thought. When they were through, she lay in the dark feeling the hurt between her thighs. Turning on her side, she eventually fell asleep. When they awoke, she asked him his name.

"Henry Sloan," he told her.

"I'm Harmony Sargent."

He took her again, twice that morning.

Harmony stayed with him for one month. She never once left the shack. She was afraid of the other blacks in the neighbor hood. Every night and sometimes during the day, Henry had sex with her. Harmony loved the way Henry made her feel. When he wanted sex, no matter how he wanted it, she gave it.

Even though she was semi-happy with Henry, she was tired of the deceit and loneliness that were plaguing her. She was ready to come clean, to bare her soul in hopes her family would take her back.

One morning after a hot round of sex, she told him.

"I have to go, Henry."

"Why, I though we had something."

"We did, but it is time for me to leave."

"I'm going to miss you."

"I'll miss you too," she said, giving him a soul kiss.

CHAPTER 37

Another year passed. It wasn't as easy as Sherry had hoped it would be to forget Ralph, the father of her son. At three years of age, Gerald was very much like his dad, so much so, it made it difficult for her to forget Ralph.

Even as hard as she tried, the nights were the hardest. Memories of their love-making all but kept her awake. Once in a while, she had to resort to relieving herself to enable her body to relax.

It had been a little over three years since the last time she had been with a man. Her need was great, but so was her willpower. If Ralph would just come home, she would forgive him for whatever he did. The Lord knows she has not done everything right in her thirty-six years.

What was it that she did so wrong to make Harmony want to hurt her so badly?

What bothered Sherry the most was the fact that Harmony would just disappear without a word. Did she do something to drive Ralph into her sister's arms? Was he with Harmony now? Did Ralph run off with Harmony, or did something else happen?

Even the private detective she hired wasn't able to find them. How could they stay hidden for so long? It seemed as if they had dropped off the end of the earth. After three years, she let the detective go. He wasn't worth the money she paid him.

Besides, she thought, I still have Vanessa, my parents, my son and my business. Vanessa might be Ralph's blood sister, but she was more like her own sister and not just a friend. Especially now that Harmony has done everything she could to ruin her life.

Thinking of Vanessa made Sherry smile. Sherry wasn't dating, but she wasn't moping around the house either. Thinking and worrying about Vanessa's brother was another story. She knew a man in her life was what she needed right now. She couldn't do it.

Vanessa was out on one of her so-called dates. She dated out of boredom, not because she liked the guys. All the guys Vanessa dated were ignorant nerds and out for one thing, and she knew it. Men can surely be jerks sometimes, she thought. At twenty-seven, she was still a virgin. Many times, she wanted to find out what sex was like, yet she never found anyone worthy of the feat.

She was still too young yet; what was the hurry, Vanessa thought. Trying to find someone like her brother wasn't easy. Ralph had hurt her, yes, but she knew deep in her heart that wherever Ralph was, he still loved her. Maybe someday, some year, Ralph will let her know where and how he is.

Vanessa was in the back row of the drive-in, necking. Sam had managed to cop a feel now and then. His actions irritated her, but to stop him from whining, she let him have his kicks.

This time, Sam had progressed from going through her clothes to a bare breast. The feel of his hand on her nipples brought back old memories of the one night she made a mistake and got in bed with her brother. This didn't feel as good or as exciting as it did that night.

On that night, if she and Ralph had gone any further, they would have made love. As much as she knew she would have loved it, she knew it would have destroyed him. He believed in right and wrong too much to do that. Yet, he did do it with his Harmony. She wasn't his blood, maybe that was why.

"Spend the night with me, Vanessa," he said as he began sucking her nipple.

She was thinking so hard about that night with her brother, she wasn't paying any attention to when Sam pulled her breast free of her bra. When she realized that it was Sam sucking her nipple, a yearning began to surge through her body. Instantly, she knew Sam's groping had gone too far.

"I'm not ready for that sort of commitment yet."

Pushing away, Vanessa said as she stuffed her breast back into her bra.

"Christ, Vanessa, don't your hormones give you trouble? You're twenty-seven for Christ's sake."

Tired of his whining and groping, she wanted to go home.

"Sam, I'm tired of your constant moaning when you don't get your way. You knew from the beginning I wouldn't have sex with you. Please take me home."

"You always have an excuse, and I am sick of it," he whined.

"Fine, if that is how you feel, you don't have to ask me out again."

"Don't worry, I won't."

They left the drive-in before the movie was over. Neither said a word all the way back to her house. As soon as Sam pulled his car up in front of her house, Vanessa got out of the car. Without saying a word, she slammed the car door to emphasize her displeasure. Briskly walking away, she never looked back.

Chapter 38

It was a cold, rainy night when an old, beat-up pickup pulled into a local motel, not far from the medical center. Glancing at her daughter, Harmony smiled. How peaceful Rebecca looked curled up on the seat next to her. It would be so nice to be young again. No worries, no problems and a mom who could fix everything.

Sitting in the pickup outside the motel, Harmony broke down in tears. Knowing she had thrown everything away for a night of sex with her sister's husband, she felt sick at heart. She was at one time a partner in the clinic with her sister. The clinic was a place that made her feel valuable to herself and to her family. A place where her family could be proud of what she had accomplished.

Finally shaking off the feelings of dread, Harmony left the truck and trudged to the office with her daughter in her arms. She had to bend over the child to shield it from the wind and rain.

The motel was seedy, but it was all she could afford. Harmony was tired on her feet from the lack of sleep. Having been worried about how she would be welcomed by both her sister and her parents, she hadn't slept well lately. Would she be able to face Ralph after all these years? Maybe he wasn't married to Sherry any longer. Tomorrow, most of her questions will be answered.

The room smelled musty and damp. It reminded her of the rooms she slept in with both the obese detective and the gargantuan black man. The bed, a double, stretched almost from wall to wall, leaving only enough room to get to the bathroom.

Placing Rebecca on the bed, inside the small, cramped room, she didn't bother to undress. Exhausted, she crawled between the covers. She fell into a fitful sleep, still wearing her cold, damp clothing.

In the morning, when Harmony opened her eyes, the first thing she noticed was that the room needed painting. Patches for the holes in the walls and ceiling would have to be done first.

Feeling cold and filthy, Harmony went into the small bathroom. She needed a shower, and her daughter needed a bath. The sink and bathtub were stained with rust. Seeing, she didn't have any choice, Harmony took off her soiled clothing.

Standing on the cold, worn linoleum, in front of the faded and cracked mirror, she gazed at her nude body. It was strange how having a child could change your figure. To keep her shape, she worked out frequently, yet from nursing her daughter, her breasts were beginning to sag. Her hips, which were always slim and her belly, which was always flat, now have extra flesh added to them.

Shaking the feeling of dread, Harmony took a quick hot shower to relieve the tension. All thoughts of facing her mother, father, and sister and telling them the whole truth weighed heavily on her mind.

Besides the trouble with her family, she wondered why all the men she knew wanted her for just a quick lay or a one-night stand. She was still pretty, and her body was still shapely, even with the added pounds.

Her reverie was broken when she heard her daughter cry from the other room. Once she had Rebecca handled, she got them ready for the last leg of the journey.

Chapter 39

Over the course of time, Candy and Sheldon worked on different objects, walked to different places for hours at a time. At times, Sheldon became highly frustrated. There were other times when he felt like he was actually gaining knowledge.

Each day, Candy introduced him to something new. The places and things he was introduced to began to confuse him. Once he did something, touched something or smelled something a few times, he started to catch on.

Days turned into weeks, weeks into months and months into years. It was a slow process. At times, he wanted to stop the therapy; at other times, he couldn't wait to get started.

One day, as Sheldon sat at the table across from Candy, drinking coffee, he reached for her hand and said, "Would you please come nearer to me?"

Without hesitating, Candy moved to where she sat closer to him. He was surprised at how much he had learned. Hearing the chair slide on the concrete and hearing each step she took until she was standing in front of him made him smile.

"Please sit in front of me," he stated.

Again, she did as he asked. Although Candy wondered what he was up to, she followed through with his requests.

"Did I ever tell you how nice you smell?" he asked.

"No, you never have, but thank you for saying so."

Sitting in front of him, Candy waited for him to make a move. When he finally reached for her face and touched it, she smiled. Slowly, he ran his hands over her nose, lips, ears, neck, hair, and eyes.

"You're very beautiful?"

"Thank you again."

Sheldon's progression was slow, but the results were good. He learned increasingly well, but time kept slipping by.

Day by day, Sheldon's feelings for Candy grew. At first, it was because she did so much for him, and she was his doctor. Now, after two years, he still felt excitement in her presence. Even the aroma of her body, with or without perfume, made his heart race.

Thinking more about his feelings for her, he was still leery because of their age difference. Sheldon knew Candy liked him, too, but in what way? Did she like him enough to take him on as a lover, or would she be offended and remain at a distance from him as he learned? Did he want to take the chance?

One morning, while they were sitting on the patio eating breakfast, Sheldon seemed to be lost in time. He had no idea if Candy was talking to him or not. He was letting his mind work as he tried to remember something in his past.

Losing time didn't matter to him anymore. He loved the life he was living now. Yet, little things always left him thinking. Were they of his past, or just something trivial? Sheldon had everything a man could want or need, except for a satisfying sex life.

Thinking to himself, he rationalized that he had to be still young, because he still needed a woman in his life. The only woman he knew was Candy, but she was so much older than he was, she might not be receptive to him.

Nevertheless, he made up his mind to find out.

CHAPTER 40

It was on an early Sunday morning. Outside, the weather looked and smelled and felt like rain. A cool breeze was blowing through Vanessa's bedroom window. Borrowing deeper into the warmth of her blankets, she drifted back to sleep.

Sherry had just sat at the kitchen table to relax and drink her coffee alone. She loved the solitude for a short while until Vanessa got up. Feeling the coolness and the peacefulness early in the morning let her relax just a little.

Suddenly, the doorbell rang. Startled, Sherry quickly got out of her seat. Then, hurrying to the door, before whoever it was rang the bell again. Opening the door and not seeing anyone, she poked her head out. Looking in both directions and still not seeing anyone, Sherry immediately thought, some of the local kids were playing a prank on her.

Seeing the newspaper lying on the porch, she had to step out onto the porch to get it, where it lay close to the railing. As she bent to retrieve the paper, she heard a strange noise come from around the corner of the house.

Immediately, the hair on her neck prickled. Frightened, she took a deep breath to scream if needed, but found her throat was dry. When nothing moved and sound was gone, she found a little more courage to venture further. Swallowing her fear, Sherry slowly moved toward where she had heard the noise. After a couple of steps, she again began to lose her nerve.

Seeing a sudden movement, from around the corner, Sherry stopped dead in her tracks. A scream was forming in her throat. Fear was making her skin prickle and her hackles rise. Recognizing the person responsible for her fright, Sherry gasped. Standing by the rose trellis was her sister, Harmony.

"Hi Sherry," Harmony said, in a low hoarse voice.

Immediately, Sherry felt that old hatred seep into her body.

"What do you want?" Sherry snarled, "Haven't you done enough damage already? What do you want this time?"

Anger and mistrust erupted from inside her. She wanted to lash out and hurt Harmony, as Harmony had done to her a few years ago.

"Can I come in?" Harmony said. "Please."

After careful thought, Sherry said, in a flat voice, "Okay, but be careful of what you say."

Stepping back in fright, as she didn't trust her sister. As Harmony made a move to cross the porch, a little girl came from behind her. The little girl must have been three years of age and looked like she was starving. What caught Sherry's attention was how the child looked. The little girl was the spitting image of her son, Gerald and husband, Ralph.

"I can't blame you for not wanting me near you, Sherry. I have done some terrible things to you," Harmony said.

Ignoring what her sister had said, Sherry got down on one knee to face the little girl.

"What's your name?" Sherry asked.

Without speaking, the little girl shrank further behind her mother.

"Her name is Rebecca, and she's three." Harmony uttered.

"Where is Ralph?"

"How would I know?"

"Rebecca is his daughter, isn't she?"

"How can you tell?"

"Gerald, could you come here for a moment. I want you to meet your little half-sister."

Four-year-old Gerald appeared from inside the house. Harmony knew beyond a shadow of doubt that the two children were brother and sister. No two children could look so much alike and be only cousins.

"There is no use in trying to hide the fact, is there!" Harmony said, and began to sob.

"No, there isn't. So please, don't make things worse by trying to lie to me again," Sherry hissed.

"I won't lie to you, ever again, I promise. I've already done more than enough damage to our relationship as it is."

"Your promises aren't any good around here, Harmony. So, tell me, if you can ever tell the truth, when did this betrayal happen?"

"It happened the night you were in the hospital having your son."

"How could it? You were with me."

"After I left you, I went to your house and seduced him. He was so vulnerable, it was easy."

"How did you know I had a son?"

"I read it in the paper the day you delivered."

"You bitch. I was in the hospital delivering my husband's son, while the two of you were fucking your brains out. What makes it worse is the fact that you, my only sister, could do something like that to me and have a child with him, too."

"It wasn't like that, Sherry. Let me tell you what really happened."

"That would be nice," Sherry chuckled with hate, "But why should I believe you now?"

"Because for the first time in my life I will be telling the truth, baring my soul in hopes that one day you will forgive me."

"This should be good," Sherry snarled.

Deep down, Sherry wanted to know everything. If she knows the real truth, maybe some of the hatred she is feeling for her sister will slowly disappear.

"That night, Ralph had no idea what I had in mind. He was elated that he was going to be a father, and you were the mother. He really loves you, Sherry. If he didn't, he wouldn't have run from me."

"And that is supposed to make me feel better? I'm supposed to condone his actions, or yours for that matter?"

"I know you're hurt and angry. I can't blame you, but at least hear me out."

Harmony began telling her sister the whole story, from when she planned it, and why, to now, the best she could remember it. Finished, Harmony sat back, waiting for Sherry to say something.

"So, you're telling me, you have no idea where Ralph went, other than away from you."

"Yes. I swear it is the complete truth."

"Don't talk to me about honesty."

"I have no reason to lie now. The damage has been done. For me to patch things between us, I have to begin by telling the truth."

"Then, if you don't know where he is, maybe he did drown in the river."

"What are you talking about?"

Sherry filled her sister in on the events leading up to today as she knew them.

"To be honest," Sherry said, "I don't think he drowned. Until somehow finds the body, I will never give up hope he is alive."

"Please, let me help you, Sherry."

"No way is that going to happen. You stay the hell away from him."

"I said, to help you look for him. Not to steel him away from you. I have already tried that and it didn't work," Harmony she sobbing.

As Harmony began weeping again and wiping tears from her eyes, Harmony's weeping affected Sherry. Even so, Sherry wasn't about to loosen up on her sister for quite a while.

"Why should I trust you now, after all you have done? How do I know you have changed? You could be out to hurt me again."

"I could, but I'm not. We could have had a good thing, Ralph and me, but he fled after the first and only time I was with him. He must have felt so guilty for what I had done to him, he sort of went off the deep end."

"All right, let's say if what you say is true. Why didn't he come home later and tell me what happened? If there is one thing he is not, is a coward. He would have told me everything."

"Maybe in the crash, he lost his memory, or wanted to hide from shame."

"Hey, what is all the shouting going on?" A voice said, coming from behind them.

Turning, Sherry saw Vanessa standing in the doorway.

"Oh, I'm sorry. We didn't mean to wake you."

"You just said we? Who are we?" Vanessa asked, trying to see around the corner.

Harmony took a deep breath, then stepped out from behind the corner.

"Hello, Vanessa."

"You bitch," Vanessa snarled, "Where is my brother?"

Sherry had to grab Vanessa to restrain her from attacking Harmony. Guiding Vanessa to a chair at the table, Sherry made her sit.

At that moment, Harmony fell to her knees, as if she were reaching for heaven, and she wailed, "Forgive me, Lord, for I have sinned. If my sin is not to be redeemable in my family's eyes, I will understand. I destroyed many hearts. Hearts that should have never been unbroken. For what I have done, I know I don't deserve repentance, but I am willing to do my best to do what I can to right the wrongs I have done. Even if my family can't forgive me, please give me a chance."

Hearing Harmony break down as she did, Vanessa became quiet.

"Please, sit," Sherry said, shaken, "Let me fill you in on what she and I have been talking about for the last hour or so."

After hearing the whole story, Vanessa stared at them both. For a few minutes, Vanessa didn't dare say anything. Then, in a fit of anger, Vanessa said, "Then he is not dead, I just know he isn't."

"We don't know that now, do we, Vanessa?" Sherry said in a solemn voice.

"I do. He is alive, and I'll find him even if it takes me the rest of my life."

"We're going to try Vanessa. We are going to try," Sherry said, trying to console her.

"Then, you must think he's alive too," Vanessa said excitedly.

"Since he has never been found, it is totally possible," Sherry said.

After two months, Harmony realized she was pregnant. Is the child going to be white or black? She would know once the baby was born. Maybe this was her punishment.

Chapter 41

Since becoming a new person, Sheldon has never gone anywhere to meet other people. Maybe, he thought to himself, Candy would like to go out with him for dinner sometime. But then, that would mean Candy would have to pay for everything. He didn't have any money.

Because of Candy, Sheldon was learning and feeling new things all the time, every day. He was beginning to feel good about himself. His confidence was growing by leaps and bounds. His new energy was infectious.

"Sheldon," she called.

"Yes, dear," he said.

"Dear? That's a first," Candy laughed.

"Oh, I'm sorry. I wasn't thinking."

"Or maybe you were thinking along the same lines as I am."

"And that is?"

"It's been three years now, and neither of us have made an attempt to live our lives away from here."

"What does the lady suggest we do about it?"

"Why don't we go to town tonight for dinner and dancing?"

"That sounds great, but first I want to show you what I am really thinking."

"Show me?"

"Yes."

Standing, Sheldon walked around the table to face her. Giving her his hand, he said, "Come with me."

Leading the way, they walked slowly across the patio toward the back door of the house. Mentally, Sheldon would have counted each step, but now he didn't need to. Candy didn't try to release his grip on her hand, which excited him even further. She liked the feel of her hand in his.

On the way, Sheldon was contemplating on how he was going to do this. He didn't want to get her angry or hurt her by misjudging her. Just inside the library door, he stopped. Moving aside, Sheldon allowed her to pass through ahead of him.

"What are we doing in here?"

"You'll find out as soon enough," Sheldon told her.

Closing the door behind her, he locked it. Laying the key on a table nearby, Sheldon walked over to her.

"Why on earth did you lock the door?" Candy asked, bewildered.

"It's time for some more lessons," he answered.

"OK, but do we have to lock the door?"

"Please. Just bear with me."

Taking her arm, he led her across the room to the couch facing the French doors. Turning from her, he pulled the drapes. The room became dark for her as it was for him. Smiling to himself, he came back to her. Stopping inches in front of her, he took a deep breath. He could smell her and feel her presence.

"You have made miraculous strides, Sheldon. I am proud of you," she said, taking his hands in hers.

He didn't sit, but remained standing in front of her.

"Good. Now let me ask you a very personal question."

"Go ahead. Ask me anything you like."

"Why didn't you ever have children?"

The question took her back. At first, she didn't know what to say or how to answer the question honestly.

Then she blurted it out, "My husband never wanted children?"

"And you? Have you ever wanted children?"

"Me? Heavens, yes, I would have loved children. But I wanted to make my husband happy. That was the duty of a wife then."

"It's not too late to have children yet," he said softly.

"My dear, it's much too late for me to have children," she said softly, "Besides, one has to be married to have children."

"Nonsense, but if a child is what you want, let me give you one."

"Wait a minute," she gasped, "What are you suggesting?"

"That we get married."

"You're young enough to be my son. My God, Sheldon, you're probably still in your early thirties. I'm forty-seven."

"What does age have to do with any of this? Over the last three years, I have become very fond of you."

"And, I've become very fond of you too, but being fond of isn't good enough," she said, "Besides, what would other people think about a woman my age, walking around pregnant with no husband?"

"What people? If you are talking about your servants, I doubt they care whom you marry or if you're pregnant and happy."

"What about you? You are still young. You have a life ahead of you. I probably don't have that many years left, especially to raise a child now," she said stubbornly.

"That's silly. You're still young and beautiful. You would make a lovely mother for one or two children."

"You've only felt my face. You have no idea what the rest of me looks like."

"Then let me explore you. I want to relish the glory of your flesh."

"You don't know what you're asking."

"I'm asking you to let me make love with me, even if it has to be with marriage."

"I wouldn't want to marry you just so we could have sex."

"Why not, you must have needs too?"

"Sheldon, I haven't had sex in at least eight or nine years. She hesitated. At my age, I don't particularly want to try again."

"Throw away your fears. Have sex with me, just this once. I'll never ask again, I promise."

"Your very good-looking and if I might say so myself, quite a hunk. Any young woman would die to have you in her bed."

"How do you feel about that?"

"I'm not a young woman. Now, I think this conversation has gone far enough."

"No, it hasn't," he said calmly.

He grabbed her arm as she tried to go past. Turning her to face him, he pulled her against him.

"I say it has," she growled, "Now let me go."

"If you walk out on me now, how do you expect me to know what a woman feels like in my hands?"

"I'll get you a girl, any girl you want."

"I don't want another girl, a pro or otherwise. I want a woman like you, that feels and will give back the love I give her."

"You don't know what you're saying, nor do you know what you're suggesting."

"Let me explore you with my hands. I want to feel your reactions as a man touches you. It would teach me how to please a woman in different situations."

"Then let me get you a woman."

"No, the woman has to be you. I need a woman who knows me and has feelings for me as I have for her. You are my doctor and my love, and I know you have love for me too, especially after all these years together. Sex wouldn't be any good unless it was with someone you love."

"You only think you love me. It happens a lot between doctors and their patients."

"Maybe you're right, but how will I know if you don't give me the chance to find out?"

"Is that all you want? One night in bed?" she asked.

For the first time in years, Candy was having feelings she had long thought were gone. The stirring between her thighs wasn't making her think clearly, more like a teenager. She was a grown woman. Nine years was a long time to lie dormant, even if she was in her early thirties at the time.

It had been years since Candy, and she had all but forgotten the thrill of sex. Now this young man, this man she created, wants her. Candy never thought she would feel sexual stirring again, but now feelings have returned with a young man young enough to be her son.

"No. I don't want just one night, but if that is all you want, I'm willing to give you one night of pleasure for all you have given me."

"If I consent, you have to promise. No one will ever know."

"Are you saying you will do it?"

"Do you promise?"

"Yes. I will never tell anyone, I promise."

"Do not say, I didn't warn you."

Hearing her unbutton her dress, he hurriedly got out of his clothes.

"This isn't quite fair," he said, leaving his undershorts on.

"What isn't?"

"You can see me, but I can't see you."

"You'll see me soon enough, through your hands."

"I can hardly wait."

When he touched her, a shiver ran through her body, and an audible gasp was heard from deep in her throat.

"Are you cold?"

"No, it's warm in here."

Chapter 42

Slowly running his fingers over her body, he began at the shoulders, then down her arms. They felt firm and slightly muscular. Going back up her arms, he moved to her rib cage, purposely avoiding her breasts. As he slid his hands down her rib cage to her waist, he was pleasantly surprised at how small her waist felt. Maybe it was because her hips were wide and well-rounded that gave him that impression.

She keeps herself in great shape, he thought. Placing his hands on her hips, Sheldon pulled her closer to him. Instinctively, Candy put her hands on his shoulders.

"Oh my God," she moaned.

The feel of her touching him almost set him off. Moving his hands behind her, he ran them over her buttocks. They felt round, firm, and well-molded. Kneeling in front of her, he let his hands slide over her thighs to her calf, ankle, and feet. Picking up a foot, he felt the toes, then tantalizingly her further, he moved back up her thighs.

"Oh, my God," she moaned again, "You're killing me."

"Do you like what I'm doing?"

"Oh yes," she crooned, "I love it."

His touch was driving her crazy. The more he touched her, the she wanted to pull him down on the couch. She thought she had to get this torture over with. Not only was she becoming damp at her inner thighs, but her muscles were quivering with need. She couldn't believe that, after all these years, just the touch of this man's hands on her body would be enough to turn her into putty.

Sheldon was impressed by how strong her legs felt in his hands. The muscles in her thighs and calves weren't too muscular, but solid and strong. His touch made her spread her thighs a bit for balance. Her knees were beginning to feel like rubber.

He hadn't touched her sexually, yet she was quivering inside. The anticipation of touching her in this manner had given him an erection. Avoiding her vagina, he slowly brought his hands around her to her tummy. He heard another slight gasp come from her lips and a slight trembling as she swooned.

Slowly, he worked his way upward to her breasts. Purposely working around them, he could hear her main. Unable to estimate their size, he deftly cupped them to feel their weight. In his estimation, her breasts were very large and heavy. Sliding his palm over the tip of her breasts, he crossed her nipples. Again, he felt a tremor and heard her cry. Her nipples already extended and felt like large gumdrops.

"Please, I can't take much more of this," she cried.

When she began to sag, he pulled her against him. As she crumbled, he caught her in his arms and picked her up. In his arms, he felt her arms slide around his neck. To him, even though she was considered a large woman, she felt light as a feather. Carrying her to the couch, he softly deposited her on her back. When he attempted to stand, she pulled him down to her.

"Enough already, I can't take any more," she moaned, "Make love to me, damn you."

His face was inches from hers. Not caring any longer, she pressed her lips to his in a desperate attempt to get her way. Her mouth tasted sweet, and her tongue soft as it entered his mouth. His emotions were high, but his resistance was gone. Wanting to explore her further, he put it off until later, for her sake.

Stepping back, he finished undressing. When he was naked, she pulled him down until his full weight covered her. Lying on her soft, lush body, he felt her limbs embrace him.

"When we are finished, and if there is another time," she panted in his ear, "I am going to explore you. You are going to know the torture you have just put me through."

Reaching between them, she found him. It has been many years since she last had a man. Quickly raising her hips, she took him deep. The pleasure was excruciating. She wanted it to last forever.

Finished and exhausted, they remained locked together. She needed to relish in the rapture he had given her. So many years have gone by, and she didn't want him to leave her just yet.

"This has to be the only time we do this, you know?"

"If that is the way you want it?" he said.

"To be honest, we should have never done this at all."

"Are you sorry?"

"No, but we can't let it ever to happen again."

"I thought I just heard you say you wanted another go-around to get even with me for the way I made you feel."

"Since then, I've been thinking it would be a mistake."

"I will respect your wish. But now I have to say, you will be wasting your incredible beauty by squandering a sexual appetite we both can enjoy for many more years to come."

"You might be right, but it wouldn't be right to lead you on."

"Why would you be leading me on?"

"Because this was a mistake," she said, standing.

When she left him, he remained on the couch listening to her dress. Minutes after she was gone. With her gone, he did the same.

Two months after making love, Candy knew she was pregnant. Seven months later, she gave him a baby girl. Sadly, Candy had just given birth to a beautiful baby girl, but now she lay in her bed dying.

Sheldon sat by her side, holding her hand. Tears streamed down his cheeks. His heart felt heavy with his loss. Being blind, Sheldon had no idea how he was going to take care of the child. He still had the servants, but that wasn't their duty. They had their own jobs to contend with.

Just before her final breath, Candy made Sheldon make a promise.

"Please promise, you will name our daughter Melissa."

"I promise. Now, stop talking and save your energy."

"There isn't much time left," she murmured, "My only regret is if only we have enough time to perhaps have another child," she said.

Her eyes fluttered. Her strength was waning quickly.

"I would have liked that too. I love you, Candy."

Smiling, she said, "I love you, too, Sheldon."

Her hand went limp, and her eyes clouded over as she passed into her New World.

Chapter 43

Vanessa was in her third year of college. It was her goal to be a doctor, like her adopted sister Sherry. In the last few years, Vanessa had many long talks with Sherry about her brother. She also asked Sherry how she copes with being a doctor and a single parent at the same time.

For the last five years, since her brother disappeared, Vanessa has been very angry, lost, and confused. The only three people she could trust were Sherry and her Sherry's mother and father, but Sherry was the only one Vanessa could confide in.

Sherry was ten years older than Vanessa, but Sherry loved her more like a sister than she did her real sister, Harmony. By spending most of her time with Sherry, Vanessa became interested in medicine too.

At first, Vanessa helped around the office with filing or typing. Sarah, Sherry's secretary, was more than willing to teach Vanessa all she knew. Soon, Vanessa ended up having additional duties, such as supplying the clinic with needed items. Many times, Sherry allowed her to dress in greens and watch procedures first-hand. Never once did Vanessa get in the way.

Vanessa enrolled in the junior college nearby. Her goal was to get all her minor and preparatory classes out of the way. When the time came, she would transfer to the medical school of her choice. That way, Vanessa could concentrate solely on her chosen profession. For the next two years, with fifteen units per semester, Vanessa had little time for anything else.

When Vanessa came home for summer vacation, she was sitting at the table with Sherry. They were relaxing over a cup of coffee and reading the morning newspaper. Page by page, Vanessa read only the articles that appealed to her. She was skimming through the ad section when an ad caught her eye. It happened to be the day off from the clinic for Sherry. Harmony was on call.

"Sherry read this," Vanessa said, handing her the ad section.

Even though the beginning of her childhood wasn't much fun, Vanessa had always wanted children. Her brother Ralph was the reason she wanted children. With him, life had been good, and it would be again once they found him.

Immediately, Vanessa put all thoughts of school behind her. Seeing the ad, she quickly decided that this was what she needed to pass her time until she went back to school or got married.

"Are you thinking of answering the ad?" Sherry asked.

"It would be perfect for me during the summer."

"That's up to you, Vanessa. If you take the job, you will have to decide what you want to do about your schooling. Will you continue school or take time off?" Sherry asked.

"I'll have to ask him if arrangements can be made for me to have time off to attend classes," Vanessa replied.

"What will you do if he won't agree with your terms?"

"Then, I won't be able to accept the job."

"Where is this place?" Vanessa asked, putting down the paper.

"The place is somewhere on the other side of the canyon," Sherry told her, "You don't have to do this job, you know. There is plenty of money to go around now."

"I know there is, but this is something that interests me. I want to at least look into it."

"It's your decision. I'll back you in whatever you decide."

"Thanks, Sherry, I knew I could count on you."

"Do you want me to go with you to the interview, if you get one?"

"Of course, I do. I need your support."

"First, I have to check in with Harmony at the clinic. Call me and I'll go with you."

Chapter 44

Stunned, Sheldon sat holding Candy's hand long after it was over. Willing her to return to him, he bent over her and kissed her. He still couldn't believe his Candy had died after giving birth. She was such a strong woman, so vibrant. He remembered the three days she remained out of his bed.

After that one time, Candy vowed never to get into his bed again. She was bound and determined not to have sex with Sheldon again.

Each one of those nights, Sheldon lay in agony wanting her. Respecting her wish, though he didn't want to, he remained in his own bed.

Then, three days later, she came to him.

"Damn you. I can't hold off any linger," she said, sliding in next to him.

"I was hoping you couldn't," Sheldon said, taking her into his arms.

Giggling like a child, Candy quickly joined with him, spending the full night wrapped in his arms. The next day, at her request, he moved into her room with her. They never married, but that didn't seem important any longer. Just being together, enjoying a full life together, was enough.

When she told him she was pregnant, Candy couldn't believe how giddy both were about the baby. She had always wanted children but had given up hope when her husband refused to have any.

Then fate struck. Sheldon came into her life. Sure, he was thirteen years younger, but he made her feel younger, too. They would frolic in bed like teenagers, even after Candy became pregnant. She had lost so much time without sex; she wanted to make up for lost time.

No one knew what would happen. As far as the doctors were concerned, she was healthy and should have delivered a healthy baby. She did, but something went wrong, and Candy died. Now he was a blind single father with a small child to rear.

Finally, when the doctor came into the room, Sheldon dropped her hand. Moving away from the bed, Sheldon began to openly sob. The doctor closed her eyelids, then pulled the sheet over her face. The sound of the sheet moving told Sheldon that at last everything was final.

All the servants stood in the background. He heard the women crying. He was sure the men had their heads bowed, too. As the doctor left the room, Peter spoke.

"Mr. Sheldon, sir, may we have a word with you?"

"Of course, Peter. What can I do for you?"

"We know this is a bad time, sir, but we are all wondering now that the Mrs. is gone, God blesses her soul, if we still have our jobs?"

"Of course, you do, I'll need all of you, more than ever now. Besides being like family, you're all very good people. I would love for all of you to stay on if you so choose."

"Who will watch the child?" Emma, the cook, asked.

"I guess I'll have to hire a nanny or nurse to do the job."

"Until you do, could I possibly do the job?"

"Of course, but who will do the cooking?"

"My husband has always helped me. Now I will help him until you find someone suitable to watch the child."

"Thank you, Emma. I appreciate your concern."

"We all love you, Mr. Sheldon. We were so happy when you took the Mrs. as your bride. She was so happy. If she could have only lived to see the beautiful child the two of you produced. We are pleased you asked us to continue."

"Thank you all so much. Seeing as today is ruined anyway, you are all released of your duties for the rest of the day."

"How will you eat?" Emma asked.

"I'll manage."

"If it's all right with you, sir, I would like to finish my job today, as if nothing happened," she stated.

"Yes." A chorus of voices said behind her. "We will all finish the day. Time off is not what we need at this moment." Peter said.

"I thank you all from the bottom of my heart, but there is one request."

They stood waiting for him to continue.

"Since we are as a family, please leave the Mister off and call me Sheldon. Other times, when we have guests, you can call me Mr. Stevens. Calling me sir makes me feel too old, and I'm a long way from being old."

Laughing, they said, "Very good, Sheldon."

Everything went smoothly. Emma was good at her word and did a great job with Melissa.

On the morning of the next day, after a hard night, the cry of a baby awoke him. At first, Sheldon lay in bed trying to figure out who was crying. Then it hit him. It was his daughter Melissa. Scrambling from his bed, he rushed to the nursery across the hall.

"It's all right, sir, I have her," Emma told him.

Emma had beaten him there. Sheldon moved to where the voice came from. He could hear the sounds of the rocker as Emma rocked his daughter. Standing by the chair, he listened to his daughter as she took her nourishment. That night, before going back to bed, Sheldon prepared an ad for the paper the next day.

Nanny or nurse wanted for full-time work. This person must be able to live at this address. Anyone interested should contact Sheldon Stevens at 644-7788.

Sheldon started his interviews early that morning. Each person he interviewed for the position had different reactions to his condition. Most of the reactions were about his touching them. They thought it too personal for them to allow him that freedom. His request seemed unusual, and many of the applicants refused to meet the conditions, feeling it wasn't necessary.

Smiling to himself, he thought. I have a feeling I am going to find it difficult to find a good person for the job.

Chapter 45

Earlier in the week, at the clinic, Sherry and Harmony continued to have long talks on life in general. Sherry wanted to know the direction her relationship with Harmony was headed. She had to admit lately, some of her first-hand experiences she and Harmony were having had helped somewhat to patch up their relationship. Even though Sherry could not totally forgive or trust her sister, she did allow Harmony back into the clinic, but not as a partner.

Harmony moved into the same apartment house as her sister to be closer to her. She wanted to be available to help with the children if her sister ever needed the help. Instead of doing things behind her sister's back, Harmony became more open with her ideas and problems. Gerald, now seven, and Rebecca, who was six, became closer as brother and sister. Hector, Harmony's black child, was almost one.

Their arrangement was that, each morning, Sherry would take the kids to school on her way to work. Evenings Harmony would pick the kids up, including Hector, from the daycare center and bring them home.

After Sherry left for the clinic, Vanessa called the number in the ad and asked for Sheldon.

"Hello, this is Sheldon."

"My name is Vanessa. I read your advertisement for a full-time nanny. I am very interested and would like an interview."

"Do you have any experience?"

"None as a nanny, but I have taken care of three children that are not mine," she replied.

"Are you married?"

"No, sir, I am a student in Medical school."

"How old are you?"

"My age is twenty-eight. If you will give me a chance, I know you will not be disappointed."

Sheldon liked the girl because of her voice and her apparent honesty. Once he met her, he would be able to talk more about her.

"Why don't you come out for an interview, say this Saturday morning around noon?"

"I would love too. Would you please give me your address?"

"There is one other reason I need a nurse or nanny. I am blind. If that, for any reason, is a problem, tell me now."

"That will definitely not be a problem. Are there special instructions or needs, I will be required to know in order to qualify for the position?"

"Yes, there is. I'll be required to touch your face. It has nothing to do with what you look like. I want to know what kind of a woman you are."

"You can tell that by touching my face?"

"Yes. Facial features and expressions can reveal a lot about a person's personality. That and among a few other things is how I base my decisions."

"What other things?"

She could hear him laugh to himself over the line.

"No, it does not require you to sleep with me to get the position. Nor will I presume you feel you have to. The other things I have referred too are your voice and mannerisms."

"I am sorry. I didn't mean what it sounded like."

"I know you didn't. I just wanted to clarify my statement. Will I still be seeing you tomorrow?"

"Yes, I'll be there around noon tomorrow. Oh, would it be a problem if my sister came with me?"

"Not at all, I'm looking forward to seeing the two of you tomorrow."

After Vanessa hung up, Vanessa remained seated a little longer, pondering if she had made the correct decision.

I hope I'm doing the right thing, Vanessa thought. There is something about his voice that makes me feel things I haven't felt in a long while. In fact, since Ralph disappeared.

That night, when Sherry got home from work, they sat for some small talk. Vanessa related to Sherry what was agreed upon between her and Sheldon. Sherry called Harmony to explain why she was taking the next day off.

In bed that night, Sherry wondered if what Vanessa was doing was the right thing. In the morning, Sherry arrived at the clinic after dropping the children off at school to see Harmony.

"Harmony, I'm going with Vanessa for a job interview now."

"How long will you be gone?"

"Just the day, I hope."

CHAPTER 46

After the last interview was over, Sheldon began contemplating his next move. Then he thought of the new girl who would be coming later this afternoon, with her sister.

Let's hope Sheldon thought after seeing more than a dozen applicants, none of which worked for him.

The name of the girl coming was Vanessa. If he remembered correctly, she was willing to allow him his request, but only if her sister were present. Even so, Sheldon liked something about the girl's voice and her attitude.

In the back of his mind, Sheldon had already decided on Vanessa. She would be the right girl for the job, providing she agreed to work to his specifications. He was surprised at himself for making such a hasty decision before actually seeing the woman.

Before making his final decision, Sheldon would still need to touch her face. It was the only way to know more about her. What was he going to do if this person didn't work out either?

Anxious to get started, early the next morning, Vanessa and Sherry started the long drive for the interview. They had to drive through the canyon, where they had lost the man they loved. Sherry hadn't driven through the canyon in years, though she did enter it to get to her island. The island was still dear to her heart. It was the place where she met the man of her dreams.

Vanessa clearly remembered the trip she and her brother made so many years ago. There weren't any restaurants or places to stop along the way.

Entering the canyon, Sherry drove slowly, afraid the two of them would share the same fate Ralph had. When they reached the spot where Ralph's car had plunged through the railing, they stopped. For a time, they gazed out over the water, then at the railing, where the old twisted ones had been replaced.

So many years ago, Sherry thought, so much lost time. She often wondered if they would ever find Ralph. To her surprise, she realized she believed as Vanessa did. Ralph was alive, but living a different life somewhere. Where he would be living is still a mystery, and why didn't he call?

Finishing the drive, Sherry drove through the shore town that Vanessa and Ralph passed through so many years ago. Once they crossed the bridge to the town on the other side, they headed back upriver. Driving upriver, Sherry saw a few large homes in the distance.

"Could one of these huge homes be where they were headed? Sherry said.

"Ralph and I had wondered what those houses would be like, the time we came through this area," Vanessa said.

A half-hour later, they decided to stop for breakfast.

"We have time, would you like to stop for something to eat?" Sherry asked.

"That sounds like a good suggestion. Who knows how long it will be before we get another chance to eat?"

Arriving at the address the man had given them early, Sherry pulled up to the gate. Brick walls, twelve feet high, surrounded the property. A gate, with thick iron bars, barred them from entering the grounds. At the gate, Vanessa pushed a button.

"State your name, please," the voice said.

"Sherry and Vanessa Sergeant," Sherry answered.

"State your business," the voice said.

"Vanessa Sergeant is here for an interview."

When the gate swung open, Sherry drove through. The spacious driveway wound its way to the mansion. Both sides of the driveway were littered with colorful flowers and overhanging trees. At the house, the driveway ended in a circle, part of which was beneath a large canopy. In the center of the circle, a small garden, with several varieties of roses, grew around a magnificent marble fountain.

Parking the car, they sat for a while in awe as they gazed at the magnificent surroundings. This man must have a lot of money, she thought. He must have a huge crew to keep this place looking so beautiful.

CHAPTER 47

Getting out of the car, they slowly made their way to the front door. Climbing marble stairs, they came to huge double oak doors. A giant chandelier hung overhead. At night, the light would light the entire entranceway. Just as Vanessa reached for the knocker, the double doors swung open. An older man, dressed casually, answered the door. Vanessa could see the man wasn't blind.

"My name is Vanessa Sergeant, and I'm here to see Mr. Stevens."

"Come right this way. Mr. Stevens is in the library, waiting for you."

Leading the way, the man ushered them into a huge library filled with thousands of books. A tall blond man was standing, looking out the door with his back to them. On first sight, both Vanessa and Sherry stood still in shock. The man's body structure was identical to Ralph's. Unable to see his face, they waited for him to turn toward them.

The man gave the appearance that he had been peering out the two large French doors at the scenery before him. From what Sherry could see, the view was more breathtaking than the view in front of the mansion. With the doors open, a gentle breeze blew in.

As the blond man turned to greet them, both Vanessa and Sherry were in awe at how very handsome the man was. Sherry surmised his age to be about thirty, but what really drew him to her was his massive upper body. Golden blond hair and bronzed skin made the sunglasses seem out of place. Wearing a white cotton shirt and gray slacks, over penny loafers, the color of ox-blood gave him a wealthy appearance.

"I'm sorry for the inconvenience. Please come in," the man said, stepping toward them.

"You must be Sheldon," Vanessa said.

Mistakenly sticking her hand out to him, she felt foolish, so she quickly pulled her hand back. Immediately, a smile crossed his face.

After a slight hesitation, she said, "I'm Vanessa Sergeant, the woman you talked too yesterday about the nanny job."

When he extended his hand to her, she took it. His hand was huge, surrounding hers in a soft grip. She was astonished at how small her hand felt in his.

"It is nice to meet you, Vanessa. Now, who is the other person with you?"

"She is my sister, Sherry."

"Nice to meet you, too, Sherry." He said, taking her hand.

Sherry is a smaller woman than Vanessa, he thought.

"Likewise, but how did you know there was more than one of us?"

"Your sister told me you would be coming with her. Besides, I could feel your presence."

"Please excuse me for a moment," he said. Turning to the French doors, he closed them, leaving the draperies open. Turning back to the women, he suggested where he wanted them to sit. He seated them in front of the French doors. Sitting, they waited for Sheldon to take his seat, near the rear window.

As they waited for him to begin, the girls gazed at the layout of the room. The entire back wall was a solid sheet of glass. A sliding glass door was the only fixture on the wall. Sheldon waited for a moment, letting them enjoy the view and relax. Tall spruce trees, following the line of the property, grew almost all the way to the river. The river wound around a steep mountain on the other side, toward the sea.

Sitting in front of the woman gave Sheldon the opportunity to know where they were sitting without asking. Because each woman gave a different scent, he separated them by the aroma their bodies gave off.

"Vanessa, do you mind if I call you, Vanessa?" he asked,

He had turned toward her. It was as if he could see where she was seated.

"No, sir."

"Good, because you came, I assume you're willing to extend my final request."

"Yes, I am," Vanessa said firmly.

Sheldon liked people who were strong, firm and not afraid to make quick decisions.

"Would you also let me touch you, Sherry, as part of the request?" he asked.

"Yes, please do," Sherry told him.

"Great. Now, which one of you would like to go first?"

Vanessa started to rise.

"Please, don't move. I will come to you."

"How did you know I was moving?" Vanessa asked.

"The sounds you make, Vanessa. Being blind, my other senses become more acute."

"What did you hear?" Vanessa asked.

"The couch gave as you got up."

"How could you tell where we were sitting?" Sherry asked in astonishment.

"I placed you there."

"No, I mean, how did you know I was sitting on the right and not on the left?"

"I can tell by your perfume."

"How could you possibly know what perfume I wear?" Sherry said, becoming more in awe of him as each minute passed.

"I didn't until the two of you passed by me."

"We only met a few minutes ago, how could you possibly?" Vanessa returned.

"That was all the time I needed. When we shook hands, I knew your fragrance. Any other fragrance would have to be the other person."

"What if we wore the same perfume?" Vanessa asked.

"Then, I would have asked a quick question to you to find your sitting arrangement."

"It is very clever, how can you remember all that?" Sherry asked.

"I've been trained. Without such ability, I would be lost."

"You are an amazing man, Sheldon," Sherry said, shaking her head in astonishment.

Smiling, he said, "Shall we start?"

"Whenever you're ready," Vanessa told him.

Deftly walking around the coffee table, he knelt directly in front of Vanessa. Reaching toward her, he placed his hands softly against her cheeks. His touch was soft and gentle.

Vanessa became aware of his scent. It was manly, not too sweet, not too strong.

Slowly, she let his fingers touch all parts of her face, starting at her cheeks. He hesitated during his touching. There was something familiar with her features, like he had seen it touched them before. Moving slowly, he touched her nose, her eyes and forehead. Then quickly to her chin.

His touch brought back memories of her brother. How could this man and my brother have the same touch? Vanessa wondered. It's as if they could be the same people.

Smiling, he moved over to Sherry, touching her in the same manner. Again, he had to hesitate. He felt toward Sherry as he did toward Vanessa. How can this be? Finished, he stood, then walked back to his chair. He didn't tell them what he had felt.

"The two of you are very beautiful women, but I don't think you are actually related."

"Thank you for the compliment," Vanessa said, "And you are right, we aren't blood sisters."

"You, Vanessa, are very young. I would say middle to late twenties. Sherry, you must be at least ten years or so older."

"You're very blunt. How can you tell this by just your touch?" Sherry asked.

"Like I've said, I've been trained. Since I can't see you, I had to learn other ways of communicating," Sheldon replied.

"You're a very remarkable man, Sheldon. May we call you Sheldon?" Sherry told him.

"Yes, you may and thank you. Now down to business. You have the job, Vanessa, if you still want it."

"When do you want me to start?"

"You could have started today, but I know you can."

"Can I see the child?"

"I'm sorry. Of course, you can. Come this way."

At the nursery, Sheldon picked up the baby, handing her to Vanessa. He listened as both women held and talked to her. He knew then he had made to right choice.

"She's so beautiful. How old is she?" Sherry said.

"She is two weeks old."

"What is her name?"

"Melissa."

"Where is her mother?" Vanessa asked.

"She died, giving Melissa birth."

"Oh," Vanessa gasped. "How terrible that must be for you."

"This is why I need you."

"Where will I be sleeping?" Vanessa asked.

"Follow me."

Opening a door, connecting both rooms, he motioned them to enter. The room was not only spacious, but it was cute as well. All the decorations were totally feminine, with frilly pink curtains and a bedspread that matched. The canopied double bed sat near the window.

Walking to the window, Vanessa looked out at the beautiful view of the front yard from a different perspective. She immediately knew she would love living and working for this man.

CHAPTER 48

For the first couple of months, Vanessa found it difficult getting up every time Melissa cried, in the middle of the night. One night, as she sat feeding Melissa, Vanessa thought about Ralph. So, this is what he had to go through with me. How did he do it and still go to school the next day? She could hardly make it through the day, even when she didn't have anywhere to go.

Once Vanessa got used to a routine, she found that Melissa became easier to handle. Melissa started sleeping longer, which made Vanessa happy. Life went on for the three of them.

When school began, Vanessa would arise early to feed, change her and play with Melissa, until her father got up. Sheldon seemed to be a creature of habit. He would get up, go to the patio for coffee and wait for Vanessa to bring his daughter to him. Before she left for school, Vanessa made it a practice to spend time having coffee with Sheldon.

Once Vanessa left for school, Sheldon would take over caring for his daughter, with Emma's help. Emma would play with Melissa until Vanessa returned later in the day. When Vanessa was gone, Melissa became fussy. Other than that, Sheldon found it very quiet around the house.

Sheldon began enjoying the little noises made by a family. He often wondered what his real family was like. He began to wonder what it would be like to be married to a woman like Vanessa and have a few children. Sheldon missed her when she was away at school.

The first time Sherry came to visit Vanessa was at school. Emma was with the baby, trying to get her to take a nap. Answering the bell at the main gate, Sheldon was surprised to hear Sherry on the loudspeaker.

"Sherry," he said, excitedly, "What a pleasant surprise."

Pushing the button, the gate opened. Going to the door, he stood outside waiting for her. Hearing her car pull in and park, he listened for the car door to open and close. Sheldon couldn't help but smile when he heard her footsteps approach him.

"It has to be Sherry," he said.

Opening his arms for a friendly hug, Sherry quickly stepped into his embrace. Loving the smell of him, she would lay her head on his chest.

"I know, you can tell by the aroma of my perfume."

"Yes, and other smells."

"Other smells?" she gasped.

Laughing, he said, "Your skin and your hair have separate aromas."

Releasing her, they entered the home. Closing the door behind her, Sheldon led her to the patio. Immediately, Peter brought her a cup of coffee. With no need to speak, they sat sipping coffee and enjoying the others' company. At this time of the day, it was peaceful and relaxing.

What a shame, Sherry thought, to be living in such a beautiful place and not be able to enjoy the view.

"I guess there would be no hiding from you," she said.

"Why would you want to hide from me?"

"I wouldn't. That is why I came to see you."

"I wish I could see you," he chuckled.

"Why would you want to see me?"

"No particular reason, other than I just like you and want to be near you."

"What a nice thing to say."

"Like you, I say what is on my mind."

"That's funny. My husband always said things like that."

"Are you married?"

"Technically, yes. My husband has been missing for eight years."

"He's missing?"

"Yes. Something happened that wasn't his fault. He blamed himself and left."

"You never divorced him?"

"No. We have a son and I still love him, but its time to get on with my life. I will never forget my husband and will always love him, but I do need to find another man to make me happy."

"Would you like to talk about it?"

"Someday maybe," she said, "What about you?"

"I don't remember anything of my past life."

"Maybe someday it will all come back to you."

That was the beginning for both of them.

Every weekend, Sherry drove over to visit him. They found their relationship beginning to blossom. On the visits, Sherry longed to bring her son with her. One day, as she was leaving, Sheldon gave her a key.

"Use this key when you come. It will let you in the gate and into the main house."

"Why would I need a key? You will be coming here, won't you?"

"Of course, I will," Sherry told him.

"Well then, I want you to feel free to come and go as you wish, without me having to let you in."

Sherry quickly became comfortable and well-liked within the household. Letting herself in with the key Sheldon gave her, she felt she belonged.

One morning, after letting herself in, she walked across the room to the patio door. Seeing Sheldon sitting at the patio table, she slid the door open.

"Good morning, Sheldon," she said.

Rising, he said, "Good morning to you, Sherry. Do I detect other little persons in our midst?"

"Nothing can get by you, can it?" she laughed.

"Not if I can help it."

"Sheldon, meet my son Gerald, he's eight. This is my sister's daughter, Rebecca and my sister's Hector, who is one."

Stooping down, Sheldon held out his hand to the children.

"What's wrong with him, Aunt Sherry?" Rebecca asked.

"You mustn't ask things like that, honey. You could hurt someone's feelings."

"I'm sorry, mister," she said.

"It's all right, Rebecca. I am blind, but how else would you learn unless you ask questions, right?"

"How did it happen?" Gerald asked quickly.

"Gerald," Sherry said with a warning voice.

Sheldon held up his hand to silence Sherry.

"I don't rightly know," Sheldon said, "All I know I awoke up one day lying in a bed, upstairs in this beautiful place. At that time, I was in worse shape than I am now. My doctor wasn't sure I was going to live."

"Do you still see the doctor?"

"Not anymore, she died recently."

"I guess you miss her, huh?"

"I miss her terribly, but she gave me a gift before she died."

"Can we see the gift?"

"Of course, you can. Follow me."

The children followed him to the baby's bedroom. Bending over, he picked up Melissa to show the children.

"This is my gift."

"That's a baby."

"Yes, we weren't married, but she gave me this child before she died. After she died, I met your mother."

"Wow," they said in unison.

That explanation seemed to satisfy them. After putting Melissa back in her crib, he stood.

"Come on, I want to show you a beautiful place."

Sheldon led them across the yard to a point overlooking the river.

"How can you see the river?"

"I see it as a beautiful picture. The smell and sounds of it tell me all I need to know."

"Do you swim in the river?" Gerald asked.

"No, it is too dangerous. That is why I have a swimming pool."

Walking them back to the patio, they sat at the table by the pool. Sheldon ordered coffee for Sherry and himself, and soft drinks and ice cream for the children.

"You said Rebecca and Hector are your sister's children?"

"Yes."

"Where is your sister?"

"She is watching the clinic while I'm gone."

"Does that mean you are both doctors?"

"Yes, we're General practitioners."

"It must be very rewarding."

"It is."

At that moment, Vanessa came through the door.

"Sheldon, I'm home."

Going to the patio, she saw Sherry.

"Sherry," she cried, hugging her.

"Aunt Nessie," the kids said, storming onto the patio.

"Gerald, Rebecca and little Hector, come give your aunt Vanessa a hug and some kisses."

The children ran to her. It had been a long time since Vanessa had been able to hug and kiss them. Standing, she looked at Sherry.

"I'm so glad you brought the kids. I miss them," Vanessa cried.

"Yes, it's been a while, so I thought maybe you would like to see them," Sherry said, "They have missed you too."

While Sherry and Sheldon talked, Vanessa took the kids to the nursery to see Melissa. After Sherry and the kids left, Vanessa brought Melissa to the patio for her daily visit with her father.

Melissa was growing quickly. In the last few months, since Vanessa has been Melissa's nanny, Melissa had learned to crawl. Everyone could see that Vanessa and Melissa had bonded. Once in a while, Vanessa would drive Sheldon and Melissa into town for a small treat at the local restaurant. For Vanessa, it was a thrill to be seen with Sheldon and Melissa. She liked to pretend they were a happy family.

"Why does the food taste so different at a restaurant?" Vanessa asked.

"Because it is prepared differently and it is a treat," Sheldon replied.

"Eating out, the food always tasted different from home."

Once or twice, while sitting at their table with Rebecca, they overheard remarks on what a nice family they were.

Sheldon would smile, while Vanessa would look longingly at him.

Lately, Sheldon and Vanessa have begun spending more time together. Vanessa was completely happy, while Sheldon never seemed aware of her in that sense. Vanessa didn't know Sheldon was more in tune with Sherry. He was beginning to like Sherry very much. He knew she was still married and could never love him, as she does her husband, but that was understandable.

Once in a while, when Sherry came to the house for a visit, Sheldon would be gone. There were times when Sheldon needed to get out of the house and away so he could think. At those times, Peter would drive into the country. Listening softly to the music in front, while Sheldon laid his head back and thought.

He had been having mixed feelings. Both Vanessa and Sherry would always bring up the one person who haunts them both. One was his wife, the other his sister. Some of the things they say, such as how much Sheldon reminded them of Ralph. Could he be Ralph? He didn't remember much, but now and then, he would get these crazy images.

Sheldon was aware that both women were attracted to him as he was to them. At the times he was out with Vanessa, he felt she wanted more of a relationship with him. Yet, because Sheldon didn't really know who he was and some of the things the girls said, he wasn't sure what to do, especially if Vanessa was his sister. If what they are saying is true, then he would be Sherry's lost husband.

On the days Sheldon is gone, Sherry would visit with Vanessa and

Melissa. Sherry didn't want to admit to the fact, but she was falling in love with Sheldon. She was still married to Ralph. Sherry didn't feel right telling Sheldon how she felt. His being blind didn't make any difference to her.

If Sherry were to let go and have an affair with him, she didn't know how she could live with the guilt. Yet, there was something about Sheldon that drew her to him. Something else kept her from making their relationship more than it was already.

Her marriage to Ralph was standing in her way. She knew as long as she stayed married, she would remain faithful to her husband. Since meeting Sheldon, the old sexual feelings began to return. She wanted and needed a man in her life, a physical man to satisfy her physical needs. Knowing Sheldon as she did, she knew he would respect her for that decision also.

Then there was Vanessa to think about. It was obvious Vanessa was falling in love with him too. Being single and unattached, it would be easier for Vanessa to have a relationship without guilt. But then, the other side of the story hits home. If Sheldon is Ralph, if Vanessa had an affair with him, how would she feel when she learned the truth?

CHAPTER 49

One day at the clinic, Harmony asked her sister about Vanessa.

"How is Vanessa doing these days?"

"Great, you should go out and see her," Sherry replied.

"No, I've done enough damage to her already."

"What harm could it do?"

"None that way, I just feel uneasy around her."

"Whatever," Sherry said, "She can be a forgiving person."

"What is it like where he lives?" Harmony asked.

"It's a huge estate with servants."

"How does Vanessa like it?"

"She loves it, although I think she has a thing for her boss," Sherry replied.

"I hope for her sake everything works out for her this time," Harmony said.

"I'm sure it will," Sherry told her.

She is very bright," Harmony said. "How long has it been now?"

"It has been eight years. She is getting ready to graduate Med. school next semester?" Sherry told her.

"It is hard to believe it has been eight years. How time does fly."

Harmony said.

"I know. Both our kids, except Hector, are both in school too," Sherry said.

In all reality, Sherry was falling in love with Vanessa's boss, too, but as long as Vanessa was living there and there was a chance for her, Sherry had vowed to stay away.

"I know, having a kid in school makes me feel so old," Harmony said.

"That guy you're seeing. What is he like?" Sherry asked, trying to change the subject.

"I think I'm falling in love with him," Harmony said.

"You think?"

"Yes, and he feels the same about me. This is the first time in my life I have someone who loves me for more than my body."

"What does he think about Hector?"

"He says, Hector is my past life."

"Then I'm happy for you, if it all works out."

"What about you, Sherry?"

"I guess I'm still stuck on Ralph."

"Get a life, Sherry. It's been eight years now. Find someone else to make you happy."

"I've been trying," she said, "But none of the guys I date match up to the man I truly love."

"Well, I have got to run, Pete is picking me up in an hour and a half," Harmony told her.

As Harmony walked to the door, Sherry shouted, "Have fun."

"I will," she said.

Stepping out the door, it closed behind her with a slam.

The day was moving very slow at the clinic, not many patients. With only one appointment left, she would definitely be able to go home early. Sherry prayed there wouldn't be an emergency for the next fifteen minutes.

As soon as her last appointment left the clinic, Sherry went home. Any patients requiring attention would now have to go to the emergency room at the hospital.

All the way home, Sherry couldn't keep her mind from alternating between Ralph and Sheldon. At home in bed, she longed for both of them. They were so much alike that her feelings were split between them.

CHAPTER 50

It was supper time at the Stevens' residence. Vanessa and Sheldon were sitting at the dining room table with Melissa seated between them in her highchair.

"I feel this is my family," Vanessa said, looking at Sheldon.

"You should, you belong here."

"Next year, I will have to go to graduate school, unless something comes along that I feel is better."

"You've gone too far to quit now," Sheldon told her.

"Oh, I wouldn't quit, I'll just take some time off," she replied.

"What else could be better than graduating?"

"I'd like to get married."

"Have you found someone you would like to marry?"

"Yes, only he doesn't know I exist."

"He must be a fool. There aren't too many girls out there that could hold a candle to you."

"That's kind of you to say."

"It's the truth."

She started to laugh again. Not knowing what to say or do, Sheldon looked at her in a puzzled way.

"Why the frown? Is something bothering you?" she asked.

"Why were you laughing at what I said?" Sheldon remarked.

"At that moment, you reminded me of my brother."

"How do I remind you of your brother?"

"Had. I think he died in a car crash about eight years ago."

"I'm sorry to hear that."

"It's funny how many times you will say or do something that will remind me of him."

"It was meant to be."

"The two of you are so much alike, if you aren't the same person, you could have best of friends."

"You're full of flattery tonight."

When Vanessa didn't comment, silence filled the room.

"Did I say something to offend you?" Sheldon asked.

"No, it's just that..."

"What?"

"I don't know how to say this."

"Just say it. It's the easiest way."

"I think I'm falling in love with you."

"Why would you fall in love with me? There are so many healthy men out there you could pick from?"

"You're healthy. You just can't see."

"That should be enough. Wouldn't you like someone you could enjoy the same scenery with, or read with or watch television with?"

"I've been living with you for almost four years now. I think I know you, besides, all that other stuff doesn't matter to me."

"It should matter. Even if my handicap doesn't matter to you right now, it might later on, and you will grow to resent me."

"How can you say that, after all we have been through in the last four years?"

"You know what I am like here, but you have no idea who I am."

"I think I do."

"How could you? I have no idea who I am," he replied.

"What do you mean you don't know who you are?"

"I'm not really Sheldon Stevens."

"Then who are you?"

"I haven't a clue. Candy, Melissa's mother, found me down by the river eight years ago."

"Eight years ago?"

"Around there. Candy was a plastic surgeon. She repaired my broken body. Without her, I would have died, and I surely wouldn't be like I am today."

"You have no idea who you are or where you came from?"

"No."

"I lost my brother about that time."

"Where did you lose him?"

"We lost him about fifty or sixty miles up the river."

"What happened?"

"His car crashed into the river. The same river you were found in," she said.

"That is strange. Candy told me she had no clue where I came from. She also said there were no reports of any accidents in the area."

"Where his car went into the river, it wasn't found for at least three weeks."

CHAPTER 51

It was a busy day at the clinic, with more patients than time. All four doctors would be working late into the night. Sherry was happy. Tomorrow was her day off. She wanted to spend some quality time with Vanessa. It had been a few months since the last time they had been together. Earlier, Harmony came to work on cloud nine.

"What is with you, Harmony?" Sherry asked.

"I'm engaged," she said.

Doing a little dance of excitement, Harmony held out her hand so her sister could see her ring.

"Can you believe it?" Harmony sang, "I am actually engaged."

"That's great. I'm happy for you. When is the big day?"

"Three months from now, on September 30."

"That doesn't give me much time to prepare for your wedding."

"It might be my wedding, but I'm going to help."

"You are not helping," Sherry told her. "Don't worry, it will be done."

"After all I have done to you in the past, why are you still willing to help me with my wedding?"

"Because you are my sister, and you said it yourself. The past is in the past."

"I really love you, Sherry," she said, in a choked voice. I was such a fool all those years ago," she continued, wiping the tears from her eyes.

"It's over, let's put it behind us," Sherry said, hugging her sister.

Vanessa was sitting in the family room watching television. Tomorrow, she will be leaving for graduate school. She wondered why Sheldon had never tried to make love to her. They have been living in this house together for more than four years. She had made herself available to him by dropping him a few hints now and then. With only one more night here, it only gives her one more attempt to get Sheldon to make love to her.

It was getting late. Sheldon had already gone to bed. Turning off the television, she quietly made her way to her upstairs bedroom. At the top of the stairs, as she walked down the hall, she began to plot.

Wondering if Sheldon was still awake, Vanessa stopped in the hallway. The door to his room wasn't far from hers. All she had to do was go to him. It would leave him no doubt about what she wanted.

Wanting to go to him, but afraid of being turned away again, she quickly changed into her bathing suit. It was a cool night, but the pool was heated. Swimming was something she had been doing a lot of lately. By lapping the pool at an exhausting pace, Vanessa found it a little easier to tumble into bed and sleep soundly.

Tonight was different. Although she felt exhausted from her swim, her need for Sheldon wouldn't let her rest. After the swim, her need was still there and growing. In her room, she changed from her wetsuit to a silky teddy. It showed all her curves to the fullest.

Even though Sheldon can't see her, the idea is still sexy. Smiling to herself, she began running her hands over her body, especially her breasts. Between her thoughts and her touch, her puckered nipples heightened her arousal. God, I need that man, she moaned. Suddenly, she began shuddering with need.

"Damn," she moaned.

Thoughts of sneaking into his bed stimulated her further. Once she was in his bed, he would know how much they wanted each other, and he would make love to her. Maybe he is shy and does not want to make the first move.

Unable to handle her pent-up passion, Vanessa took off her teddy. Slipping into her light robe, she remained nude beneath. Silently stepping into the hall, she walked the few feet to his door. Putting her hand on the knob, she stopped. Hesitating just outside his door, she felt her heart pounding. Thinking he might hear her coming, she hesitated for a moment to allow her time to change her mind.

Slowly opening the door, she stepped into its darkness. Closing the door behind her only made the room darker. Unable to see where she was going, she held her breath in fear of bumping into something. She had never been inside his room before. She had no idea where he placed things.

Standing still, she listened for his shallow breathing. As her eyes began to adjust to the darkness, she moved slowly toward the bed. His shallow breathing suggested he was still sound asleep. Reaching the edge of the bed, she hesitated once more. Swallowing her pride and letting her body do the talking, she dropped her robe. Standing beside the bed, her body began to shiver with excitement.

No man, except her brother, had ever seen her naked. Not even her brother has ever seen how mature her body has grown. Getting into bed naked, with a man other than her brother, will be a new experience for her, too.

Still standing next to the bed, looking down at his sleeping figure, Vanessa began having second thoughts. Still, she wasn't sure if she could go ahead with her plan. Her indecision made her listen to his breathing a while longer.

Then, making up her mind, as a full-grown woman and a virgin at twenty-eight, she was sure tonight she would finally get rid of her unwanted baggage.

Never before had she had the desire to make love with any man, except her brother. Vanessa hoped her brother never knew how close they came to making love that first night after that cold swim.

Many nights, after that one night, Vanessa could still feel her brother's hands as they kneaded her breasts, then slid down her belly to cup her private parts. That night, she wasn't supposed to be in his bed. That night, if Ralph had pursued her a little harder, she wouldn't be a virgin today.

Because making love with Ralph could never happen, she never told him of her true feelings. Now Ralph was gone, and she regretted not having sex with her brother at least that one time.

Now here is Sheldon, a man she could truly love. Was she doing this because he reminded her so much of her brother? That was a sick thing to think, yet she had always looked for someone like Ralph. No one ever matched up to her brother.

Carefully lifting the covers, Vanessa slid into bed next to him. Sheldon was lying on his side facing the far wall. Pressing her full body against his back, she waited, afraid to move. The warmth of his body touching hers made her weak in the knees. She was glad she was lying down.

She could get very comfortable lying next to Sheldon every night. With her body pressed tightly against his back, she reached around him. The instant she grasped his penis, it grew in her hand. Feeling his penis grow larger and harder, she became aware of the dampness between her thighs.

She began to stroke him. This was another thing that reminded her of her brother, his size. They felt the same, and she had never forgotten. Vanessa wondered then and now, how she would be able to take such a size inside her body. It must truly hurt.

Her fondling soon made Sheldon begin to stir. She had in her life held two penises in her hand. One was her brother's. That was the night they almost committed the sin. The softness of tissue on something so large and hard intrigued her.

Now breathing heavily, he suddenly rolled toward her. His arms moved to enfold her. She had to raise her body slightly to allow his arm to go beneath her. She could hardly believe her luck. He really wanted her. As if in a dream, his soft, clinging lips pressed to hers. His breath smelled sweet. Instantly, thoughts of her brother filtered into her memory. Again, something else reminded her of her brother, his breath. Slowly, one of his hands came between them to fondle her breast.

Vanessa closed her eyes, letting pleasure sweep over her. When he tweaked her nipple, erotic feelings surged through her body. Small charges began jerking her body, making her want more as one hand fondled her breast, while the other slid between their bodies. Slowly, his hand moved down to her flat stomach, then to the pubic area. Wet with anticipation, Vanessa realized only one man had ever touched her like this. Her brother.

As if she were still in a dream, Vanessa rolled to her back. Feeling his hand cup her femininity, she parted her thighs for him. At his touch, her resolve shattered. It was too late to stop him now, even if she wanted him to. Suddenly, she felt a finger begin its journey inside her body. God, if his finger can hurt this much, she could only imagine how his erection will feel.

It wasn't long before his hand was gone, and his body moved over her. Feeling his weight push her down into the mattress, she sighed. Feeling him slide between her thighs, Vanessa grasped his erection again. Tentatively, she placed him against her wet opening. After a slight penetration, he stopped.

"Candy, you came back," he whispered.

As he slowly started his descent into her hot body, something inside Vanessa's mind clicked. Immediately, her body stiffened, but it was too late. As she caught her breath, she felt a twinge of pain as he took her virginity. Her boy tightened its grip on his erection as he filled her.

"What?" he said, as he pulled out, coming to his knees.

"Why didn't you stop me?" He asked.

"When you called me Candy, I tried, but it was too late", she sobbed.

Vanessa knew Candy was the mother of his child, but by Sheldon's mentioning Candy's name, while taking her virginity, took away her desire.

"What the hell? Oh my God, what have we done?" Sheldon said.

Rolling from her, his erection quickly dissipated.

"I wanted you, Sheldon," she said.

Staring at him with tears running down her cheeks, she said, "But, I want you to want me too, not Candy."

Stunned by what had happened, he ignored what she said. "Vanessa? What are you doing in my bed?"

"I came to make love with you."

"We can't do this," he said.

"It's too late now," she said.

He was fighting himself. Once more, he was growing an erection.

"Why not? This will be my last night with you, and I love you. No one will ever know what happened but the two of us."

"It is not right. You are so young and beautiful. You need to find someone who would appreciate you. Give your body only to the person you marry."

"You can't be that much older than I am," she told him.

"I really don't know how old I am."

"You don't look so old. Besides, I wouldn't care if you were fifty. All I know is, I love you and would marry you no matter how old you are."

"I love you, too, Vanessa, but not the way you love me. Having sex, just to have sex, isn't a good way to know how great sex really feels."

"Before I marry, I want to know what it's like to be a woman."

"You don't want someone like me. I could be your brother."

"I thought we ruled that out."

"In a way we did, but how would you feel if someday you found I was your brother?"

"Actually, you have already taken my virginity, how can you stop now? If you are my brother, I will feel lucky to have known you in this way. Not many sisters get or want that chance."

Not wanting to hear more, Sheldon became stern, yet managed to keep his voice calm, as to how he felt. He didn't want to hurt her feelings, yet he knew that was what he was doing anyway.

"Why don't you go back to your bed and forget this ever happened?"

"Don't you want me, now that you have been in me?"

"More than you'll ever know."

"Then take advantage of that fact. You have already taken my virginity. Now I want to know how making love really feels."

"No, I can't do this, please go back to your bed."

"Your hard again, damn you."

"If I knew it was you, I wouldn't have gone this far."

"Damn you to hell. You had your chance, now you will regret it. Someone else will take what you're not man enough too."

Without another word, Vanessa flew from his bed, taking her robe with her.

Chapter 52

Early Monday morning, Sherry was at the table having a cup of coffee while reading the newspaper. It was a habit she got accustomed to, soon after Ralph disappeared. This time it was for a better reason. She had to see Vanessa before she left for school. Besides, it was a chance to see Sheldon again.

Sherry hated to admit it, but she was glad Vanessa was leaving. Maybe with Vanessa gone, she would have a better chance with Sheldon. It became apparent that Sheldon wasn't interested in Vanessa the last time she visited them. Yet she knew how Vanessa felt about him. Sherry didn't want Vanessa to say someday, she interfered with her life. She could well remember the hurt feelings that came from the treachery of a loved one.

The sun was just peaking above the trees as she left her home. It was going to be a beautiful day. She could feel it. By the time the day became hot and humid, she would be inside her car with the air conditioner going. At Sheldon's, she wouldn't need an air conditioner. There was always a cool coastal breeze coming off the river.

The drive to Sheldon's home always brought her passed the place where she lost Ralph. Each time Sherry came to the place they found Ralph's car, she would slow to gaze out over the river. An hour and a half later, she was turning into Sheldon's driveway. The main entrance to the mansion was busy with activity. Servants were loading a car, parked beneath the canopy. Realizing Vanessa had not departed yet, she let out a giant sigh of release.

Parking behind the parked vehicle, Sherry got out of her car and jogged quickly to the front door. Sheldon and Vanessa were just coming out of the house. It was evident that there was trouble between them.

"Sherry, I'm so glad you made it," Vanessa said, moving toward her with her arms outstretched.

Both had smiles on their faces. They hugged and kissed each other.

"I wouldn't have missed you for the world," Sherry told her.

"I'm glad. Now I can go with good conscience."

She and Sherry hugged and cried. After kissing each other goodbye, Vanessa got in the car to leave. Sherry realized Sheldon hadn't joined them. He remained on the verandah listening to them chatter and cry.

"You had better hurry, Vanessa, or you will miss your plane," Sherry told her.

Knowing she didn't want to miss her plane, without another word, Vanessa started the engine, then drove away. Although her feelings for Sheldon, he left a pain in her heart. Vanessa knew the pain had to be placed on the back burner for the time being. In order to do that, she had to leave; to stay would only cause more heartache.

After all these years, Vanessa was going back to school to finish her schooling. This time, when she returned, she would be a doctor.

Feeling emptiness inside her, Sherry watched Vanessa go. She would miss Vanessa, but knew it would only be for a short while. Tears flowed down her cheeks as she watched the car pass from sight. The last picture Sherry would ever recall was Vanessa waving goodbye from the back window of the car.

Turning, Sherry moved toward Sheldon. Even from a distance, she could see tears streaking his cheeks. Today was indeed a sad day for all.

"Hello, Sherry," he said, in a sad voice, "How are you feeling?"

"I'll be fine, once I settle down."

"Would you like to come inside for some coffee?"

"I would be delighted. It has been a long time."

Walking up to him, she took his hand in hers. Clasping their fingers, they turned toward the door. As Sheldon led Sherry through the house, Sherry was still amazed at how comfortable he was in his own environment.

"Please sit with me," he spoke.

Ushering her to a seat at the table, Sherry settled next to him. He looked at her in such a way that it was impossible to tell he was blind.

With a smile on his face, he said, "I am so glad you decided to stay. I've been thinking about you and miss your visits."

"That's funny, I've been having the same thoughts," she replied.

"Do you think about yourself often?" he asked, chuckling.

"What? Oh, get it. You like teasing me."

"I always liked a little joking between friends."

"Are we friends, Sheldon?" Sherry asked.

"I would like us to be," he said.

"Good. I was hoping you would say that."

"I would like more if it were at all possible," he said.

"What are you saying?"

"Think on it. If you can't figure it out, it won't work."

Not sure of what to say, Sherry sat staring at him. As she took a sip of her coffee, a slight breeze made the outdoors a little more comfortable to be in.

He is a very good-looking man, but could she handle a man with no sight? Could she, if it were Ralph, have he lost his sight? Yes. For Ralph, she could and would do anything. This man, though, seems to be very independent. Would he remain that way if they were to marry? God, what was she thinking? He really hasn't said he loved her yet.

"Can I ask what you're thinking?" Sheldon asked.

"What? Oh, I'm sorry, I was a million miles away."

"You must have been about your husband."

"What would make you say that?" she asked.

"It's funny, but last night something happened that brought old memories to me."

"What sort of memories?"

"I'm not sure. It was something I can't explain yet."

"Do you want to talk about it?" she said.

"Not yet. Let's see they recurs."

"That's understandable," Sherry said.

Before they knew it, time had slipped by, and it was past noon. Feeling hungry, Sheldon ordered lunch.

"I hope you are hungry, because I took the liberty of ordering lunch for the two of us."

"Oh, thank you," she said, "I was getting hungry."

A cool wind began blowing in their faces.

"Let's eat inside where you will be more comfortable."

"That would be nice. It is getting a bit chilly," she said.

For some reason, they found themselves very relaxed around each other, for the first time in a long time. Breaking the silence, Sheldon said, "It is a long drive back. Why don't you spend the night?"

"I couldn't possibly."

"Why not? We could talk some more and get to know each other much better."

"I have to get to work early."

"Call, tell them you're having car trouble and you'll be late getting back."

"You want me to lie?" she said.

"Only, if it will help me to keep you here tonight."

Laughing, she agreed. Besides, it would be fun staying in a house like this.

She called her mother.

"Mother, could you get Gerald tomorrow, when Harmony brings him home?"

"Where are you?"

"I'm at Sheldon's and I'll be spending the night."

"Don't tell me," Her mother said.

"No, Mother. I'm not staying to have sex."

"Why not, for god's sake. It has been a long time for you, hasn't it?"

"Yes, but I'm not ready for that yet."

Hanging up the phone, she went looking for Sheldon. She found him in the library listening to music and relaxing. Sheldon sure is an interesting man, she thought. So much had happened to him in the last few years, yet he seemed genuinely happy. Still, at times, she could see the sorrow in his face. Most likely for the times and places he couldn't remember. Sharing their thoughts and dreams came easy to them, as if they had been friends forever.

Chapter 53

Six months have passed since that chance meeting between Sherry and Sheldon. She wasn't having any problems getting used to his company. Each weekend, she would drive to his home at his request and bring the children with her.

Because Sherry took the kids on the weekends, Harmony started giving more of her time to the clinic during the day as payment she thought she owed her sister. Nights belonged to Peter, unless she was called in on an emergency.

One day, as Sherry was driving to see Sheldon, thoughts began bombarding her. I'm not getting much younger, and Ralph has been gone for nine years now. Maybe I should think about starting a new life with Sheldon if he wants me. There have been days when he has all but told her so. Maybe I'll bring up the subject this weekend.

At forty-three, Sherry knew it was time to start having fun again. It has been more than twelve years since the last time she was with a man. Gerald is twelve, Ashley is eleven, and little Hector is seven.

With time passing so quickly, Sherry swore that this would be the weekend she would be making a few changes in her life. Turning into Sheldon's driveway, she suddenly realized she had not heard a peep out of her kids for quite a few miles. Stopping at the front door, she looked back at them. They were lying together on the back seat, fast asleep, holding each other like little lovers.

"Okay, kids, we're here now," Sherry said.

She watched the three children open their eyes. They seemed so innocent. Semi awake, they smiled as they sat up. Groggily, the kids slid from the car. Sherry held their hands as they walked to the front door. Before she could open the door, Sheldon opened it for them. Melissa, Sheldon's eight-year-old daughter, stood with her father holding his hand.

Coming together, the four kids jumped with excitement as Sherry and Sheldon hugged. Seeing the four kids together, Sherry was stunned at the close resemblance.

God, they look so much alike that they could be siblings. It has to be a quirk of nature, or is this man I'm falling in love with is really Ralph?

Even with her thoughts formulating, neither of them could piece anything together. Sherry and Sheldon turned their attention back to each other. Letting everything slip from her mind, except where she wanted to be, in Sheldon's arms, she sighed.

As the kids went into the house to play, Sheldon and Sherry took advantage of the kids' absence. Their lips met in a warm, soft, inviting kiss. After the kiss, Sherry felt warm and cuddly all over.

Keeping her arms around him, Sherry lay her head on his chest, emitting a deep sigh. Sherry felt like she was in heaven, feeling Sheldon's arms holding her tight. Neither of them wanted to let the other go. The children had long been out of the room.

"Can you spend the night with me?" he asked brazenly.

Laughing, she said, "I can't believe it took you six months to ask me?"

"You will sleep with me?" he said excitedly.

"I've wanted to sleep with you for a few months now."

"What about your husband?"

"It's been twelve years. I think its time to let go."

With their arms around one another, they entered the house.

"If I would have known for sure you how you felt, I would I would have asked you sooner," he teased.

"You would have known tonight. I had plans of seducing you," she said, in a low, sexy voice.

"Maybe we should forget about waiting and indulge right now."

"What will we tell the kids?"

"They're playing and won't miss us. If they need anything, Emma is always available."

Without another word, they escaped to his room. Sherry watched Sheldon undress. His body looked so powerful, so viral. The sight of his masculinity was enough to get her excited. Having seen only one other penis, when she saw the size of Sheldon's, she thought of Ralph, but didn't feel guilty.

That weekend, they slept together for the first time. Little did they know sleeping together was not new to them. During the entire weekend, they made love frequently, at times furiously. At times when the children weren't underfoot, they would sneak away for a little more pleasure.

Sheldon began having memory flashbacks. None of them, like the others he had, didn't make sense yet. They weren't long enough to have any continuity. Memories began coming more frequently, especially when Sheldon was doing things he used to do as Ralph.

Sheldon never realized he was doing those things. Because he didn't, he couldn't tie sequences together. They were all very short sequences of places and people he couldn't identify. Afraid of being made fun of, he kept everything to himself.

Confusion would keep him awake nights, usually when being bombarded with small flashbacks. The flashbacks would suddenly wake him. Startled, he would sit it up and stare into the darkness. At times, he would have to get out of bed to wipe sweat from his body. Sherry would awaken with him. Taking him in her arms, she would hold him until he could relax and fall back to sleep.

Sunday morning, just about the time Sherry and the kids were ready to leave, Sheldon stopped them at the door. A look of concern crossed Sherry's face.

"Sherry, would you and the children please join me in the living room for a moment?"

"Sure," she said.

As everyone followed him into the living room, Sherry wondered what could be so important. Instead of asking, she held the question inside and waited.

"Would everyone please take a seat?"

Each of them took a seat near the other.

"There is something I want to ask all of you."

"All of us?" Sherry said.

"Yes. I want to know how the children would feel when I ask you to marry me."

"You would be our daddy?" they asked simultaneously.

"Yes. And your mother would be Melissa's mother too."

"Goody," they shouted.

"Are you going to ask her?" Gerald asked.

Turning to her, Sheldon kneeled then said, "Sherry, would you marry me?"

"I'll have to get a divorce first," she said.

"Will you marry me, after you're divorced?"

"I thought you would never ask."

"We'll talk more about its next weekend, when you get here. Meanwhile think about it. We'll begin making plans next time."

Being on cloud nine, the drive home seemed to go quickly. By the time Sherry and the kids got home, Sheldon started having second thoughts about marrying her.

After they left, he began having more memories, more like flashbacks that scared him. Lately, he was beginning the put people and places to mental pictures.

In his memory flashes, Sheldon saw Vanessa in small sequences that didn't make sense yet. Sherry was among the memories, along with another woman he couldn't place. At times, Sheldon saw images of some cabins, somewhere in cool places, where there was water. Other memories were of a smelly, damp shack and an old, rusty car. To Sheldon, none of the memories seemed to tie together.

At times, he would think about different people, but they were never together. They were just memories coming to him from nowhere special. Nothing made sense, but he knew somehow everything was connected. Because of these memories, he would suddenly become frightened.

It is not the time to make a mistake and marry the wrong person. First, he had to know who all those people were and how the places were connected. How can he tell Sherry how he feels without hurting her? How can he tell her that he thinks about different faces and places, none of which make any sense? Deep in his heart, Sheldon knew he loved Sherry, but right now, he wasn't sure that was enough.

During the week, while Sherry was at work, Sheldon began having thoughts of Vanessa. She hasn't called him once in the past six months. He was beginning to worry. Did he make a mistake by not making love to her that night? What is Vanessa to him anyway? Were they married before the accident, or is he her brother?

For sure, they have slept together, but he couldn't remember ever having sex with her. Short sketches of those images confused him. None of the sketches gave him a clue about what really happened on those nights.

What was Sherry to him? Remembering a lot of good times and remembering seeing her in the hospital were all the clues he had of them together. They were always together on those good times, but why was she in the hospital?

There was another woman in the picture, too. At the moment, he had no idea how she fit in, or who she was, for that matter. Whoever she is, she had to have something to do with all this. Before saying anything to Sherry, he would have to be exactly sure what he was going to say.

Chapter 54

It was the day of Harmony's wedding to Peter Coleman. When Sheldon arrived, Sherry met him at the car. Upon getting out of his car, Sheldon immediately took hold of her arm. Turning toward his chauffeur, he said. "Samuel, please sit in the car and wait for me."

"Why don't you send him home?" Sherry said quietly.

"I'll need a ride home after the wedding."

"I thought you would want to stay here with me?"

"That isn't too good an idea at this time."

"Why isn't it?"

"Your parents will be here, and I don't want to be in the way."

"That's silly. We're consenting adults. Besides, it isn't the business of anyone what we do or don't do when we are together."

"I don't agree. I am blind and need familiar settings."

"Well, I'll be with you the whole time," she said.

"You know I don't want to be dependent on anyone, especially you."

"Is that how you feel all the time?"

"No, just when were away from familiar surroundings," he said quietly.

"You will have to trust me on those times."

"I do trust you, but I also want you to mingle and have fun."

"Having fun for me is to mingle with you. I love you, Sheldon, and I am proud to be seen with you. Now stop being self-righteous and let me help you."

"You are right, lead on."

Before the start of the wedding, Sherry ushered Sheldon around the room to meet her parents, then her sister Harmony.

For some reason, meeting Harmony bothered Sheldon more than meeting her parents. He couldn't see her, but he could see her, but for some reason, he could sense something about her that bothered him. It was strange. Why didn't he get those vibes from anyone else?

When Sheldon shook hands with her father, there was something about him that seemed familiar. Harmony, on the other hand, stirred him deeply the other way. Her perfume and voice made his senses soar.

Could Harmony be the mystery woman in those memory flashes? If so, what did she have to do with all of this? There wasn't any doubt he had met her somewhere before. Because he didn't know everything yet, he put it aside for a while. Whenever he and Sherry were together, Sherry never talked about Harmony.

Sherry held Sheldon's hand as they moved around the yard. She introduced him to many people, both family and friends. Everyone seemed nice and eager to meet him. In the midst of a conversation with one of the men, Sheldon heard a bell chime in the background.

"It's time for the wedding, Sheldon. We best take our seats," Sherry told him.

With Sherry on his arm, she steered him to where he thought was the outside aisle. The only voices he could hear were on one side only. He knew when they reached the front, because the voices were now behind him.

Taking a seat next to Sherry, they waited for the service to begin. Others filed in next to them. He recognized Cathy by the perfume she wore when they were introduced. Soon the music began, yet small talk continued around him. All the women were commenting on the bride's maid and the other girls in the wedding.

Then the church became deathly quiet, except for the wedding march. It was time for the bride to begin her trip down the aisle. From what Sheldon could hear, from the women around him, the bride must have been very beautiful.

After the wedding, as everyone began to file into the reception hall, Sherry again steered him in the right direction. Even with Sherry as his guide, Sheldon felt out of place. As all the men and women watched the festivities, he sat in the dark, wishing he could join in the celebration.

Soon, it was time for the men to dance with the bride. Sherry never left his side, which made him feel terrible. Before Harmony and her new husband departed, Harmony came to him.

"Hello, Sheldon."

"Hello," he said.

"I'm Harmony,"

"Congratulations on your wedding. I imagine you are a beautiful bride."

"Not quite as pretty as Sherry, but a close second."

"I see you're a little modest," he said.

"Sherry, would you mind if I danced with Sheldon?"

"No, I'll dance with Peter."

"If you're as smart as I think you are, marry her," Harmony whispered, as they danced.

"I intend too."

"Good. She needs you in her life. You are all she thinks and talks about."

"Doesn't she talk of her ex-husband?"

"Thanks to you, she might forget him."

Soon after the festivities were over and the bride and groom departed, Sherry led him into the house.

"It's getting late," Sherry told him, "Many of the people have started to leave."

Alone at last, Sherry whispered to Sheldon, "My mom and dad have gone to bed."

"Is that a hint?" he said, jokingly.

"No, it was a statement of fact."

"When do you want to go to bed?" he asked.

Ignoring his remark, she said, "The wedding was beautiful, wasn't it?"

"Harmony seemed to be extremely happy," he said.

"Why do you say that?"

"I'm not sure yet. Give me some time."

"Give you some time for what?"

"I need time to put all these memories together."

"Have you been having more memory flashes?" she asked.

"Yes, loads of them, but none of them make any sense yet."

"Why don't you tell me about them? Maybe I can help you."

"Not yet, as I said, I need time."

"Don't you trust me enough to tell me?"

"It doesn't have anything to do with trust."

"Then why won't you tell me?"

"Why does it make such a difference to you?" he said, angrily.

Thoroughly frustrated now, Sherry suddenly didn't want to deal with his problems any more tonight.

"Maybe it would be better for you to go back home. At least until you feel you can trust me."

Chapter 55

Another six months passed. Both Sheldon and Sherry were too stubborn to relent and call one another. Though she was feeling miserable, Sherry found a lot to do with the kids and her clinic to take her mind off Sheldon.

Missing Melissa, Gerald, and Rebecca constantly asked Sherry why they didn't see Melissa and Sheldon anymore.

Sheldon missed Sherry desperately. Also, Melissa missed playing with everyone. She kept reminding her father by asking when Gerald and Sherry were coming to see them.

At nine, Melissa turned out to be a very bright child, excelling in her schoolwork. Sheldon kept putting her off about Sherry and the kids by telling her he was too busy.

"Did you and Sherry have a fight?"

Not wanting to lie to he said, "I'm sorry to say we did, Melissa."

"Won't we ever see them again?"

"We will, one day, I'm sure."

"I thought you were going to marry her?"

"We are going to get married."

"You won't, if you don't talk to her or see her."

"You're a little to smart for your own good. What you are saying does make sense. Someone has to break the silence and mend the feelings. Being a male, I guess I should break the ice.

"Call her, daddy. You won't be sorry," his daughter told him.

When Harmony and Peter returned from their honeymoon, they moved into a new house across town, taking Rebecca and Hector with them. It was a large home with four bedrooms. Every now and then, they would have Gerald stay with them. When they were together, Gerald seemed different from when they were apart. They had grown so close, keeping them apart hurt them.

"When are you coming to see our new home? Harmony asked Sherry, after a few months had passed,

"Why don't you have an open house? You can invite the family and friends," Sherry told her.

Now a full-time mother, Harmony gave up her full-time practice, except when Sherry absolutely needed the help. Peter, a top executive with his company, made more than enough salary for the three of them to live on. He wanted to adopt both of Harmony's children plus start a family of his own.

Three months after their honeymoon, Harmony found she was pregnant. Even with a new one on the way, she was worried about her sister.

"What happened between you and Sheldon, Sherry?" Harmony asked.

"We had a fight."

"Christ, everyone has fights. Whatever he did couldn't be as bad as what I did to you."

"That was different. You are my sister."

"And he is the man you love and want to marry."

"I have to divorce Ralph first, and that is not an easy task for me.

"Don't be stupid, call him, mend things up. The two of you belong together."

"You have changed Harmony."

"People do change, if they are given the chance," Harmony said.

"Not all people change."

"Maybe, they don't, but Sheldon seems like a great guy, and you use a great guy in your life again.

"Perhaps you are right. I will call him the first chance I get."

"What is wrong with right now?"

CHAPTER 56

Once Vanessa was back at school, after leaving Sheldon's home, she found she would have to take some refresher courses because of the layoff. That would take an extra two years.

At first, still hurt by Sheldon's rejection, she stayed to herself, concentrating solely on her studies.

Finding it difficult to make ends meet, Vanessa took a part-time job at a small grocery store, a few hours a week.

Now in her senior year and still a virgin at the age of thirty-three, she decided she didn't want to get married at all, but she did still want a child. Seeing what her mother and Sherry have gone through, Vanessa wanted no part of married life. If she were to have a child, she would raise the child as a single mom, but having a child would make her wait longer to get her career started.

Putting her feelings about her career aside, Vanessa decided it was time to lose her virginity. Right now, Vanessa needed and wanted someone to love more than she wanted her career. With her brother gone, she needed someone special in her life. Sure, she still had Sherry and Sherry's parents, but she wanted more out of life. She needed a man to show her the joys of sex and have a child.

One night, as Vanessa was driving home from her part-time job, her car quit running. Still a long way from town, she knew she had only two choices. One, she could walk back to town, or sit here to wait for someone to come along.

Checking all the gages, Vanessa knew she still had plenty of gas.

Getting out of the car, she opened the hood to peer inside. With no idea what she was looking for, she wished she had her brother to take care of her. While she was under the hood, a car pulled over to the side of the road just ahead of where she was stalled.

Stopping what she was doing, Vanessa saw a man get out of his car and approach her. He was an older man, perhaps twenty or thirty years older than she was. Just a nice person wanting to help, but she didn't recognize him either.

"Having problems?" the man asked.

"Yes, this damn thing just stopped running," she said angrily.

"Could I have a look?" he asked.

"Have at it."

While under the hood, he kept talking to her.

"What is a vulnerable girl like you doing out here at such an hour alone?"

"I was on my way home from work."

"Where do you work?"

"At the small grocery store, back a couple of miles back."

Not seeing anything obvious, he pulled out his head and closed the hood.

"A mechanic is going to have to look at this. If you would like, I can give you a ride to town. Then in the morning, you can call a mechanic."

"Being, I'm a Medical student, I don't have the time or the money for repairs. Besides, I have an early class in the morning."

"I'm sorry, but I've done all I can do, except give you that ride."

"I guess you're right. Can you wait while I lock up my car?"

"I'll be in the car waiting."

When she climbed into the car, she found it toasty warm. Vanessa didn't know how chilly she was until the heat in the car flowed over her body.

"My name is Roscoe Russell," he said.

"I'm Vanessa Anderson."

"You are in medical school. Are you about ready for graduation?"

"I'll graduate at the end of this semester."

"That must make you around twenty-four."

"Thanks, but I'm thirty, almost thirty-one."

"You don't come close to looking that old. Did you start school late in life?"

"Yes. I also had two years off."

He didn't ask why.

"How old are you?" She asked him.

"I'm sixty-three."

"Talk about looking young, I thought you to be around forty."

"Thank you."

"Are you married?" Vanessa asked.

"I'm on my third marriage. This one has lasted eight years now, which is a record for me. What about you?"

"Single. I haven't even been engaged. Do you have any children?" Vanessa asked before he could say anything.

"I have five children. I have a son by this wife, a son and daughter by my second wife, and two daughters by my first wife, which I haven't seen or heard from in years."

"Why all the divorces?"

"You don't want to know."

"Was it that bad?"

"Let's just say, I love a lot of different women."

"I take it you've been caught cheating."

He began to chuckle. She could tell he was sort of embarrassed. Vanessa took an instant liking to him. He could have easily taken advantage of her instead, he was very helpful and trusting.

"Have you ever thought about getting married and having children, or do you plan to just work your whole life?"

"Marriage, I don't think so, but I would love to have a child."

"You want a child without marriage?"

"Sure. In that way, I don't have to worry about being hurt."

"I take it you've been hurt before."

"Not me, but I have seen enough of it in my life to know I don't want it for myself."

After that statement, he became quiet, as if he was contemplating his next move.

"Turn right," she told him.

"Now turn left."

"Right here," she said.

He pulled over to the curb. While sitting there waiting for him to say something, she began getting nervous. It wasn't until she opened the door and got out that he spoke.

"Which apartment do you live in?" he asked.

"Number twenty-eight," she said, looking at him, "Thanks for the ride."

Surprised at how she felt, she stood and watched him as he drove away.

If he had made a pitch, Vanessa thought, I might have let him have her virginity. She was ready, and he would have been perfect. Not only was he good-looking, but he was married. From what he told her, he didn't like commitment any more than she did. He was thirty-one years older than she, nearly old enough to be her grandfather, so his age wouldn't have bothered her either.

Chapter 57

The next day after class, Vanessa called a mechanic.

"Hello, this is Jimmy's Garage."

"Hello, my name is Vanessa Anderson. Last night, on my way home from work, my car died a couple of miles out of town. I need to get it fixed."

"If you will tell me where you are, I will come get you. Then I can see what I can do about fixing the car for you."

A few minutes later, a young man driving a tow truck pulled up at her apartment.

"Are you Vanessa Anderson?"

"Yes, I am."

"Climb in," he said, opening the door for her.

On the way to her car, he didn't waste any time trying to find out who she was.

"Are you married, or spoken for?" he asked.

"No," she said softly,

Knowing where this was leading, she waited.

"How about going out with me sometime?" he said.

He was quick. She wondered if he was as fast on a date.

"I don't even know your name."

"I'm Vince Tunny."

Vince seemed like a nice person, and he wasn't bad-looking. The only problem was his age. He looked quite young.

"You do realize I am older than you," she said.

"I know. I like older women. They are more experienced. Young girls seem too silly for me."

"How old are you?"

"Does it matter?"

"Let's just say I don't want a kid."

"I'm nineteen and working my way through college."

"What college?"

"Right now, I'm in junior college."

"Where would we go?"

"Where would you like to go?" he asked.

"How about taking me to dinner and dancing?"

"I don't make much money," he choked, "Go easy."

"Why don't you get a better-paying job?"

"I don't want the responsibility."

"Responsibility comes with life."

"Responsibility only comes with marriage."

By now, they had the car on the truck and were on their way back to the station.

"I'll tell you what," she said, "I'll be at the library tomorrow night until eight. After that, we can go for pizza and a show," she said.

"Now you are talking my language."

Vince went back to work. Vanessa went to the waiting room. She called her boss from the pay phone.

"Ted, my car broke down, and I am at the station getting it fixed. I doubt I will make it to work tonight."

By the time her car was ready, it was too late to go to work. As Vanessa was pulling into her parking space at her apartment, a familiar car was parked nearby. Slowly getting out of her car, she watched as the man got out of his car. It was like deja vu.

"I thought I'd stop by to see if you needed help getting your car," he said.

"I appreciate the thought," she told him, "But I've already taken care of that situation."

"I can see that, and that's too bad. I really wanted to get to know you better."

"You're married."

"You told me you're looking for a father for your child."

"How do you know I meant you?" she asked.

"You sort of hinted. Not in so many words, but the implication was there."

"So, you would like to father my child," she said.

"It makes sense to me. You want a child and not a husband. I think you don't want a man who will to be a nuisance once the baby is born. As you know, my track record stinks. I'm a perfect candidate."

"Give me your work number and let me think about it," she told him.

That night, Vanessa lay in bed thinking. She wanted to lose her virginity, yes. But she also said it would be with the first person she dated. However, did she really want to sleep with Vince, who was fourteen years younger, or Roscoe, who was over thirty years older?

Actually, Roscoe would be the better man for the job, being he wouldn't want anything to do with the child after it was born. The only problem was, he was nearly twice her age. As far as that went, she wouldn't have to worry about Vince wanting anything to do with the baby either. Yet, because Vince was so much younger than she was, he might be more apt to change his mind after the baby comes, whereas Roscoe wouldn't.

There is one other solution. She wasn't really crazy about the idea, but it would stop her from having to make a choice. Fuck them both and let nature take its course. That way, she wouldn't know who the father was. If any question ever came up, she could tell them the other guy was the father.

The next night, Vanessa went to the library dressed for her date. Vince was on time. At least that was a plus in his favor. After pizza and a movie, Vince drove to the lake. He didn't waste any time going for it. He must have assumed she was a willing woman. The spot he picked was desolate. Driving into the midst of trees that blocked their view from the road, he turned off the engine.

"Do you like to skinny dip?" he asked.

"I have never done it, but it sounds like fun."

"Let's go. This is a perfect spot," he said.

Getting out of the car, they walked to the edge of the lake without touching.

"I suppose you take all your girlfriends here," Vanessa said.

"No, you are the first."

"Why am I the first?"

"I don't date much. There aren't too many older women around here to date."

Vince pulled his shirt over his head and dropped it on the ground. He was tall, skinny, and had a greasy look to him. Hesitating for just a moment, Vanessa thought, Oh, what the hell. She did come here to fuck him. Shrugging her shoulders, she slowly unbuttoned her blouse. Vince had stripped in seconds. Vanessa took a lot longer. Before long, they were nude and staring at each other.

"My God, you have a beautiful body," he said.

As he moved toward her, her eyes moved to his erection. It doesn't take much for him to get excited, she thought.

"You have beautiful breasts. They're so full and firm. How do you keep them so firm?"

"By not having sex," she said.

"Excuse me?"

"I am a virgin. Do you still want to fuck me?"

"How old are you?"

"I'm almost thirty-one."

"Christ, you're older than I thought."

"Does it matter?"

"No, let's swim," he said.

Wading out into the water was the hard way of getting in. Water felt so much colder when you ease yourself on, especially when it reaches your crotch. Vanessa dove in almost at the same instance as he did. Where she came up, she found she couldn't touch. Treading water, she looked for him. He surfaced not far from her.

Before long, her body got used to the cold. Without touching, they swam until the cold started to take over. Then they swam closer to shore. When they were able to touch, he grasped her hand and pulled her to the beach. The night air was cold. Goose flesh covered her body.

On dry land, Vince immediately took her in his arms to kiss her. His kiss tasted like cigarettes. His lips were tight and felt hard. His kiss was nothing like Sheldon's or her brothers, for that matter. It didn't take Vince long for his hands to go to her breasts. Cold hands made her nipples extend. Instead of kissing them, he began pinching them. The act only irritated her.

"Stop," she said.

"What is wrong?" he said, pulling away.

"Let's go back to my room, where we can get comfortable."

"Damn. You're driving me crazy," he said.

Slipping back into their clothes, he quickly drove to her apartment. Pulling into the first available parking space, they scrambled from the car. Running up the stairs, as soon as they entered her apartment, they quickly began to undress. Each item of clothing that came off stayed where it landed. Once in her room, they fell on bed.

"Vince, I think you forgot the rubber."

"Oh, baby, I can't wait."

"Either you put one on, or you go home."

"Oh fuck," he said.

Quickly, he searched his wallet. Finding a rubber, Vanessa watched as he rolled it on. Once on, he moved over her.

"Now, do it quickly." She said.

Without preliminaries, he pushed inside her.

"Shit, you hurt me."

"I'm sorry."

His thrusts were hard and desperate. He climaxed long before she was ready. Her first experience with sex was a bust. Because of this experience, Vanessa wasn't sure she would ever enjoy sex. No sooner had he finished than he dressed and left.

The next morning, after her unsatisfactory sexual experience,

Vanessa lay in bed thinking about what had happened. What she had last night couldn't be what sex is like. It had to be better than that.

Getting out of bed, she poked around in her purse until she found Roscoe's number. It didn't take him long to answer.

"Roscoe here," he answered.

"Hi, this is Vanessa."

Before Roscoe got to her place, the phone rang. It was Vince.

"Can I come over?"

"I don't think so, Vince. Your not what I am looking for."

If Roscoe wasn't any better, she would forget about sex altogether.

Chapter 58

Sheldon was having memory flashes more frequently now, but they were always the same. Jumbled memories of people and places made him think about getting professional help. Picking up the phone, he called a doctor, but backed out before he answered.

His days were spent pacing, rarely sitting for long periods of time, in any one place. His servants were beginning to get concerned. Sheldon was feeling like the house was empty. He liked it when Sherry and the kids were there. He missed them terribly, but he still had his male pride. Early one rainy morning, Melissa was moping around the house like her father was. When he paced, she would emulate him.

"Will you please stay still, Melissa?"

"I'm bored."

"What would you like to do?"

"I want to go see Gerald, Ashley and Hector."

"I don't think that is a good idea, on a day like this."

"Please, daddy, I want to see them."

Knowing he could never turn his daughter down, Sheldon caved in.

"Samuel, get the car ready," he said, over the intercom.

Five minutes later, Samuel had the car waiting with the doors open. Once everyone was in the car and seated comfortably, Samuel closed the door. A few moments later, Samuel drove out of the driveway.

"Where to, sir?" he asked.

"We're going where you took me a few months ago."

"Very good, sir," he said.

The wind was blowing quite furiously as the journey began. Soon it started to drizzle, and the roads became slick. Before long, they were moving up the river toward the canyon. Once they reached the canyon, the wind seemed to die down, but the roads remained slick from the rain.

"Samuel, would you please go a little faster?" Melissa asked, "You're going too slow."

"I am afraid to go faster, Missy," he said, "The roads are slippery."

"Please, Samuel, I want to get there."

"I can't do that, Missy."

"Do it, Samuel. Going a little faster won't hurt," Sheldon responded.

Sheldon's mind swirled with thoughts of what he was going to say to Sherry when he saw her.

"As you say, sir," he said.

Knowing better than trying to argue, Samuel managed to pick up the speed a little. Conditions of the road made Samuel nervous. Glancing in the rear-view mirror now and then, Samuel noticed both Melissa and Sheldon seemed unaware of the dangers ahead. Melissa loved to go fast, and Sheldon couldn't see the danger, but usually Sheldon would have him hold the speed down anyway.

Melissa was watching the scenery pass by. Her father had his head on the back of the seat, resting. Sheldon was again thinking of the past. More memory flashes began to bombard him. On this trip, Sheldon didn't know why, but some of the sequences were beginning to fill in. Not all, but some were beginning to make sense. He was beginning to remember more than bits and pieces.

Feeling the car swerve on the slippery road, Sheldon began to feel a little nervous. Speed never bothered Sheldon before. He was about to tell Samuel to slow down, when the car went into the hairpin curve. It was the same curve he had lost control of ten years earlier, only in reverse fashion. By the time he told Samuel to go slower, it was too late.

Samuel applied the brakes a little too hard, freezing them. When the brakes locked, on the slippery pavement, the car swerved. Fright made Samuel overcorrect. Suddenly, with the car careening out of control, it hit the guardrail.

At that split second, it was ten years earlier. The sound of metal ripping filled the air. He could picture the car going over into the river, only this time, luck was with them. The car wasn't going nearly as fast as it was ten years ago. This time, the bumper caught in the guard railing, bringing the spinning car to a crunching halt. The sound of tearing metal hit a nerve in Sheldon so hard, he nearly passed out.

In that moment, he saw the accident in his mind. He remembered a car speeding through the winding road, but from the opposite direction. When the car hit the guardrail, he remembered it soaring into the air. As the car hung over the river, he remembered the terror in his mind. A moment before landing upside down into the icy water, Sheldon felt the impact again, as if it were happening again.

In that one quick moment, Sheldon felt a load of pain shoot through his body. Then, as if he were reliving the incident, he remembered emerging from beneath the water. Sheldon could actually feel the excruciating pain as he tried to swim toward shore. Taking only a few strokes, he passed out.

Only one question entered his mind. Why was he driving so restlessly? What had made him be so reckless? In that instance, he remembered everything. Sweat rolled down his face, and he began to tremble. He heard someone hollering in the distance. As if he were now in a different world, he felt someone shaking him.

"Daddy," the voice said, "Daddy, please wake up."

Opening his eyes, he looked into the eyes of his young daughter.

"Are you feeling all right, daddy? You were screaming."

Shaken, but now somewhat subdue, Sheldon took a deep breath and then let it out slowly. Feeling more relaxed than he has for so long, he answered his daughter.

"Yes, sugar, I'm all right. I'm fine now."

Taking her in his arms, he squeezed her tightly. He felt her little body shake with silent sobs.

"You were so white and sweaty," she said, "I thought you were getting sick."

The chauffeur had gotten out of the car to check the damage. A few minutes later, Samuel climbed back into the car to start the engine. With the engine running, Samuel sat there still stunned, staring out the shattered windshield.

"I'm sorry, Mr. Stevens. I guess I lost control," he said.

"It wasn't your fault, Samuel. You were instructed to drive too fast for existing conditions. I take full responsibility for this."

"Thank you, Mr. Stevens."

When Samuel did not immediately drive away, Sheldon said.

"Are you all right, Samuel?"

"I'll be fine in a moment, sir, as soon as I calm down."

"Well, I don't blame you. I don't feel well either. I think maybe we should go back home."

"Yes, sir. That would be nice, sir."

Melissa didn't argue or cry. Shaken more than she wanted to believe, she too wanted to go home. Frightened out of her wits, she would never ask Samuel to drive too fast again. Further up the road,

Samuel found a place to turn around. The trip back to the house was quiet and serene.

Chapter 59

Lying in bed with his daughter, memories of Vanessa came flooding back. He remembered Vanessa as a small young girl. She had been lying in the crook of his arm, just as his daughter was now. Sheldon remembered he was a teenager, but his name wasn't Sheldon. It was Ralph.

Back then, because it was so hot in the room, he and Vanessa kicked the covers off. They were wearing just their underclothes. When Vanessa kissed him on the cheek, it was as if he could feel it again.

It was evident, from what he just remembered, that Vanessa is his sister. Memories began to flood him. Everything was beginning to fall into place. Seeing Vanessa as she was then made Sheldon realize she had to be only five or six years younger than he is. If she were in her late twenties now, then he had to be in his early thirties. Again, as he did in the car, Sheldon's breathing became ragged. Sweat covered his body instantly, making his body become clammy to the touch.

Aware of the change in her father, Melissa quickly came to her knees to look at him.

"What's wrong, Daddy?" Melissa asked.

Hearing his daughter talking to him, he momentarily lost the images that were flooding his mind.

"Nothing, sweetheart, you can go back to sleep now."

"You are all wet to touch," she said, "I'll go back to my bed."

"That's a good idea, honey. I'll see you in the morning."

"Goodnight, Daddy, I love you," she said, kissing him good night.

"I love you to sweetheart."

As soon as Melissa closed the door, Sheldon slid out of bed. Hurrying to the bathroom, he quickly climbed into the shower. Hot water always calmed him. This time it didn't help.

God, everything was coming back to him. He was remembering Vanessa as a young girl, in his bed. If she is his sister, why were they sleeping in the nude?

Getting out of the shower, he dried off, then in his room changed the bed. That was when another memory hit him.

He was helping Vanessa make a bed. Suddenly, he remembered explicitly what they had been talking about. Shock exploded inside him. He knew what had happened and why they slept together.

Memories came rushing back, in torrents. All the answers he had been searching for were coming back to him. It was like reading a book, only the story was his. Some of what he remembered scared him. Some made him sad. Now knowing what had really happened, how it happened and why it happened was vivid in his mind. Thinking of Vanessa, Sherry, and Harmony made him sweat. What a mess this was. Would the women forgive him for what he had done?

Hurrying to the telephone, Sheldon phoned Sherry. This was the only way. He would know if he would be forgiven or not. He had to tell his story. Did Harmony tell her side of the story, or did she tell Sherry the truth about what happened that night? The phone rang ten or twelve times. He was about to hang up when the phone was finally answered.

"Hello?"

"Hello, Sherry, this is Sheldon."

"I know who it is," she said, coldly.

"Please give me a chance. I know everything, and I'm ready to tell you everything."

"Are you sure you are really ready? I can't go through that hurt again?"

"Yes, I will tell all the truth about everything. Can you get your whole family together by tomorrow evening? I need to tell you, your sister, your parents, and Vanessa."

"Why do you want to tell my parents?"

"You will know when I tell you. Can you find Vanessa? Do you know where she is?"

"Yes, I know where she is, but she doesn't want to see you for some reason. What happened between the two of you?"

"I'll tell you when I see you, but I will only tell you and Vanessa. No one else need know everything of that went on."

"Fair enough, I will make sure everyone will be here."

"You have to get Vanessa."

"I'll get Vanessa. She has been living in the old cabins she and her brother used to live in when they first came here. Wayne, the owner of the cabins, let her stay there until all her problems were over."

Chapter 60

"Hello."

"Hi, Roscoe, this is Vanessa."

"How are you?"

"I'm fine, but I want to ask you for a favor."

"Name it."

"I've decided to take you up on your bargain, but."

"But..."

"I want to be sure you still want to be the father of my child. Maybe we can have a trial run for a while."

"That sounds like fun."

"Can you come to my apartment tonight?"

"What time?"

"You pick it. I'll be home."

"I'll be there."

Roscoe was there before dinner. Wanting to see if Roscoe was going to be like Vince and be too anxious, she purposely didn't come onto him right away. If he were like Vince, he wouldn't be the one to sire her child either. To her surprise, Roscoe was a perfect gentleman. He never tried to push himself on her. He was comfortable waiting for her to pick the time.

"Let's go out to dinner," he said suddenly, "You must be hungry."

"Yes, I am. Where will we go?"

"I know just the place."

They had a leisurely dinner, a few drinks, talked and danced a few hours. When he sensed she was ready, he asked.

"Do you still want to try that trial run?"

"Yes. I'm ready," she murmured.

Roscoe drove her back to the apartment without even trying to kiss her. They didn't run to the bedroom as she expected. He asked for a cup of coffee, which was made for him. The second night, he came to the apartment with groceries.

"Go sit in the other room while I whip up a couple of steaks," he told her. "Do you like beer?"

"Yes."

"Good, grab one and go in to watch television," he told her.

When the steaks were ready, they sat and ate like a married couple. After they had another beer, they made small talk in the living room. He didn't stay long, but before he left, he kissed her for the first time. He was confusing her. By now, any other guy she dated would have at least tried to feel her up and talk her into bed.

"Why haven't you tried to bed me yet?" she asked, after their first kiss.

"I didn't want to scare you off."

"But, you know what I want you for."

"True, but sex isn't any good unless there are feelings between the two. The partners have to have some sort of feeling for each other."

"That is good, but when I know I'm pregnant, I want you gone from my life."

"That won't be a problem."

"And you still want feelings between us?"

"Of course," he said, "I might be a cheater, but when I have sex, I want the woman to enjoy the act and beg for more."

"Want to give me a crash course?" she said.

She was ready for him to kiss her again.

"Not tonight. It's late and you're not ready yet."

"So, you say."

"I'll be back tomorrow night, when we can take our time and really get to know each other."

"I can hardly wait."

The next night, Roscoe took her to dinner again. After they put on some music at the apartment and had a couple of drinks. When Roscoe was sure she was ready, he took her to bed.

In bed, he started slowly, kissing and stroking her skin. He made her beg for him to take her. When the time came, he took his time penetrating her. Not sure of how this going to feel, she screamed with delight. He made her forget the first man who took her. Vanessa never knew sex could feel so good.

"How can any of your wives not like the way you make love?"

"My technique wasn't the complaint."

"Then what is the problem? Why three divorces?"

"Because after having babies, they got fat and fat women turn me off."

Three months later, when Vanessa graduated, they went their separate ways. A few weeks before her graduation, Vanessa knew she was pregnant. Vanessa didn't end the affair until the day after she graduated. They spent that last night together as if they would never part, but it was for the last time.

"I take it this is the end," he said, after he rolled from her.

"Yes. You are a wonderful lover and person. If I were older or you were younger and I was looking for a husband, I would have loved to be number four."

"Talk like that makes me horny again. You are a delicious young woman, and I'm going to miss you. If you decide to change your mind, call me. You know my number."

"Roscoe, I'm thirty-one, you're sixty-four. That makes you thirty-three years older than I am. You're old enough to be my grandfather."

"It doesn't bother me," he chuckled, "does it bother you?"

"After what we have done, you can ask that?"

"Then what is the problem?"

"In ten years, when you are seventy-four, I'll be forty-one. Wouldn't you be afraid I'd be looking for someone younger than you?"

"That could happen, I guess, but in the meantime, I would keep enjoying what we have had, the last three months."

"And you wouldn't cheat on me?"

"I didn't say that."

"When and if I ever marry, I don't want a man who seeks other women."

"You could always have that younger guy."

Laughing, Vanessa said, "If I change my mind, I'll call."

CHAPTER 61

Two weeks after graduating and Roscoe left Vanessa and returned home. It had been three years since she stormed out of Sheldon's life. She still missed him, even loved him, but his refusal to make love to her had hurt her more than she wanted to admit.

At home, Vanessa found the house empty. Not wanting to see Sherry just yet, she called her at the clinic. When Harmony answered, Vanessa hung up. The third person she called was Cathy.

"Hi Cathy, this is Vanessa. Do you know where Sherry is?"

"Hello Vanessa, how have you been?"

"I'm fine Vanessa said.

"You don't sound fine. Why don't you come over and talk for a while?" Cathy said, "Sherry is with Sheldon, and she has the children with her."

"Thanks," she said, hanging up.

Driving across town, Vanessa stopped to see Wayne.

"Hi Wayne, how have you been?"

"Vanessa," he cried, "You're a sight for sore eyes. It's been a long time. What's up?"

"Can I stay here for a while, while I get back on my feet?"

"Vanessa, you can stay here as long as you want too. If it wasn't for you and your brother, there wouldn't be cabins."

"Thanks, Wayne, I won't forget this."

"I see you're going to be a mother. Who is the lucky man?"

"He's just a guy I knew in college."

"Are getting married?"

"No marriage for me, marriage is completely out for me."

"Well, with what happened to you and Ralph, I guess I can understand."

Her old cabin was actually vacant. After moving into the old cabin, Vanessa and Wayne spent a lot of time together, talking and reminiscing about the years gone by.

Vanessa took over where her brother left off, running the cabins for Wayne. Both she and Wayne were happy with the arrangement. With Vanessa running that end of the business, he was free to do what he really liked. He could put all his time into running the station.

Hearing of Vanessa's return from her mother, Sherry made it a point to see her. Why did she want to live in the old cabin? Letting harmony hold down the fort, Sherry went for a visit. On first sight, she gawked.

"Who is the man?" she asked.

"Just a guy I know."

"Are you getting married?"

"No way, after what you and my mom have gone through, marriage is out."

Knowing how Vanessa felt, Sherry didn't push the issue.

"You don't have to live here, you know," Sherry told her.

"I want to be here. It brings me closer to my brother."

"You have to let go, Vanessa. I did."

"Then, I take it you and Sheldon are getting it on."

"Don't be angry with me," Sherry said sadly, "It was past time."

"I'm not angry with you. You should have changed your life years ago."

They resumed their relationship. Having lunch together again was fantastic.

When it came time for Vanessa to have the baby, Sherry stayed at her side. Steve and Cathy made themselves available if needed. Ralph was born three minutes before midnight on the first day of July.

It was still dark in the early morning as Sheldon's car pulled into the driveway. Melissa was asleep in the back seat. It was a chilly fall morning. An early morning, dew covered the ground. Leaves were beginning to fall from the trees, leaving their branches bare. Sheldon didn't have to knock. Sherry was waiting for them at the door.

"Hi Sheldon," she said, letting him in. "How have you been?"

"I've been lonesome as hell. Other than missing you, I've been just great."

"Without you in my life, I've been lonesome too. I've missed you terribly," Sherry told him.

Not able to contain herself any longer, Sherry flew into his open arms. They kissed hungrily.

"I love you, Sherry, I always have."

"I love you too. So, don't ever leave me again."

"That is a promise. Only I hope you will still feel that way, after I tell you the whole story."

"Hi, Sherry," a small voice rang out from the car window.

"Oh, Melissa," Sherry cried, "I'm so sorry. I didn't know you were here."

Rushing to the girl, Sherry gathered her in her arms.

"That was because she was sleeping so soundly in the back seat, I didn't have the heart to wake her."

"She could have frozen to death in the car."

"No, she wouldn't. Samuel has the heater going. Besides, I was going to get her up after I told you how sorry I was for not keeping you informed."

Turning, Sherry kissed him hard on the lips again. Breaking the kiss, Sherry led them into the front room. None of the kids were up yet. It was too early for them.

In the living room, Melissa said, "I'm so tired. Can I go upstairs to bed?"

"Of course, you can when you wake up, play in your room until Gerald gets up. Your dad and I are going to take a nap too."

"Together?" Melissa asked.

"Together," she told her, "It's been a long time since we have seen each other."

"You're not going to sleep," Melissa giggled, "You're going to do what parents do at night."

"Where did you get that idea?" Sherry asked.

"I'm not dumb, you know."

With that, Melissa dashed up the stairs and into Rebecca's old bedroom. Turning to Sheldon, Sherry said. "We still have a few hours before Gerald gets up and a lot longer than that before everyone else gets here."

"I hope you mean what I think you mean," he said.

"I do. Come with me."

Pulling him with her, she led him directly to her bedroom. Hurriedly undressing, Sherry moved everything on the dresser aside. Sitting on the dresser, she called him to her.

"Come here," she said, spreading her thighs. They made love quickly and furiously. Later, after a second bout in bed, Sheldon lay facing her.

"There is something I have to tell you about Vanessa, while she was living with me."

"I hope you aren't going to tell me you made love with her."

"No, we never did."

He told the story from beginning to end, leaving nothing out.

CHAPTER 62

No one said anything to Sheldon as they filed into the room. Sheldon felt like an outcast. In one way, being left out didn't bother him. He had prepared himself for it. The only person to talk to him was Harmony.

"Everyone's here," Sherry told him.

Taking her seat next to him, Sherry told him where everyone was sitting. Once he knew where everyone was, Sherry waited for him to begin his story.

"Harmony and her husband Peter are sitting on the couch. Vanessa and Ralph Jr., her one-year-old son, was next to Harmony and Pete."

"Did you say Vanessa and her son, Ralph Jr.?"

"Yes, we didn't want to tell you until we had too."

"Is the father of the child here?"

"No. She didn't marry him." Sherry told him. "Now let me finish."

"My parent's Steve and Cathy, are sitting by the door with Gerald, Rebecca, Melissa and Hector. Now that you know where everyone is, you can say what you came to say. Just remember. Whatever it is you have to say, I will still love you, and I want to stay married to you."

"Please help me up. I don't want to trip on anything or anyone."

After helping him stand, she remained standing with him, leaving her hand on his arm for support.

"When I begin, please don't interrupt me until I have finished. Nothing will be left out, and I don't want to forget anything, so bear with me."

Sherry had missed him terribly over the past few months. Now knowing what transpired between them before Vanessa left for school, Sherry felt more comfortable, but she still didn't know the whole story.

"Before we go any further," Steve said, "I want to know you're intentions with my daughter."

"Now don't get upset, Steve, please, but I cannot marry your daughter."

"You can't what?" Steve shouted.

Even Sherry heard Sheldon tell everyone he couldn't marry her, she quickly pulled her hand away from his arm. Sheldon ignored the way she pulled her hand away. He had expected she would.

"Please hear me out," Sheldon said, "When I am through, you can do what you wish."

"Let him finish, Dad," Sherry said in a hurt tone.

"How can you be so calm after hearing what he just said?" Steve roared.

"I am not calm," Sherry growled. "I am furious, but I also want to hear the whole story. He owes us that much."

When everyone finally stopped chattering, they sat and listened.

"I could never marry Vanessa or Harmony if I were single."

"Why the hell can't you?" Steve shouted again, coming out of his seat.

"Because I am already married . . ."

"You mean to tell me," Sherry screamed, "You have been making love to me, and you're already married to someone else?"

In her anger, she began pounding him on the back. Lifting his arm, Sheldon tried to protect himself from his wife's onslaught.

"Well, sort of," he said.

"Sort of, are you telling me you knew you were married to someone else and you still had the gall to make love to me?"

"I didn't say that."

"What did you say?" She shouted, hitting him again. In anger and frustration, she struck him on his arm with a closed fist.

"I just said I was already married."

"Who are you married to?" Vanessa exploded.

Holding up his hand, Sheldon tried to hold down the noise that filled the room again.

"If you weren't blind, I'd punch your fucking lights out," Steve screamed at him.

"Steve. Sit down and shut up so he explain." Cathy said, pulling on her husband's arm.

Reluctantly, Steve sat, but remained in a violent mood. Sheldon ignored the tirade. Turning toward Sherry, he said.

"Sherry, my real name is Ralph Anderson."

A loud murmur went through the room, drowning out anything else he had to say.

"You can't be Ralph; you don't look like him," Steve said.

"Yes, he could," Vanessa cut in, "I always said he seemed a lot like my brother."

Vanessa rushed to him.

"Is it really you Ralph?"

"Yes, and I can prove it."

"At a risk of getting personnel," Sherry said, "Sheldon's, I mean, Ralph's lovemaking did seem very familiar."

"You would think of that," Vanessa said, laughing.

A chorus of laughter filled the room as everyone started celebrating.

"Will everyone please be quiet?" a small voice shouted.

Hearing the voice, everyone stopped talking.

"How do I know you're really my father?" Gerald said.

It suddenly became very quiet in the room.

"Would the three of you children please come over here to me?"

Slowly and tentatively, the three children made their way to Sheldon. When they got to him, Sheldon said, "Now would you three children please turn to face your families."

Standing together, the three children left no doubt they were siblings.

"Oh my God," Cathy said. "It is you. What happened to you all these years?"

The room was silent again. Ralph started his story, not leaving anything out. First, telling them about what happened after her left the hospital. Telling them about Harmony, the telling them about his race down the canyon. From that point, he told about how his new daughter came to be. He told them about what almost happened with his sister and why it didn't happen.

Finished, he said, "If anyone has any questions or doubts, now is the time to voice them. As far as the Children are concerned, they are all mine. I take full responsibility for all of them.

Now, what is done is done," Sheldon said, "No one in this family should be ostracized for what happened. Many past actions have hurt this family, but as far as I am concerned, that is all past history. As for me, if I am not wanted, I will leave and stay gone. I will remain out of your lives forever. All I ask is that I am allowed to see my children once in a while."

"Agreed, no one should be ostracized," Steve said, "Let by gone be by gone."

"Do you really mean that, Steve?" Sheldon asked.

"Yes, I do. All of us have made bad mistakes at one time or another in our lives. If Sheldon, or is it Ralph, can forgive after every-thing that has happened to him, we should be able too also."

"What about you, Peter? Can you forgive me?" Harmony said, looking at her husband.

"I have nothing to forgive. We didn't know each other at that time. Now, I am not condoning what you did, but I am willing to forgive and forget as long as nothing ever happens like that again."

"Thanks, sweetheart," Harmony cried, "I promise on my life, I will always be true to you, and I will never do anything to you or to anyone ever again."

Everyone seemingly happy, walked around hugging and kissing. No one said anything to Sheldon about his being wanted or not. Taking his seclusion from the group as a no, he didn't know what to do, and he couldn't leave without help.

Suddenly, a hand touched his shoulder, startling him. Because of the noise in the room, he hadn't heard anyone come up to him.

"I hope you weren't thinking of going?"

"I'm not going anywhere until someone helps me out the door. I have a feeling I am not wanted any longer. "

"You are wrong, son," Steve said.

Gently pushing Sheldon into the seat, he was standing by, Steve continued, "I'll admit I wanted to kill you as you were talking, but now," he hesitated, "Now, I feel as if I have my whole family back with a few extras."

"Thanks, Steve, that means a lot to me."

"Welcome home, son," Cathy said, pulling him up and hugging him.

"Yes, brother of mine," Vanessa said, "I thought I had lost you forever."

"You would never lose me, Vanessa, especially now that Ralph Jr. is alive."

"Sherry, would it be all right if I came to live with the two of you for a while?" Vanessa asked.

"No offense meant, mom and dad," Vanessa continued, "But I need to spend some lost time with my long-lost brother."

"No offense taken," Cathy said, "We understand. Now maybe we can really enjoy retired life. No offense, Vanessa."

Everyone started laughing, but quieted when Harmony stepped up to Sheldon.

"I am so sorry for everything I did to you and Sherry. I don't really deserve to be forgiven, but because of your kindness and generosity, you have earned my everlasting love and support. Now, do we call you Sheldon or Ralph?"

"I was as much to blame as you," he told her, giving her a hug.

"No, you weren't. I instigated the whole shebang from the beginning."

"Forget it. I have. Besides, we both have someone to love from it."

"Quiet, everyone. My brother isn't finished yet," Vanessa said.

Vanessa stood next to Ralph with her arm around his waist. Sherry stood a few feet away.

"If Sherry wants to stay married to me, I would like to take both her and Gerald home with me to New Port. Everyone is welcome at our home whenever anyone wishes to visit. As far as Rebecca goes, I would love to take her with us too, but I suppose she would rather live with her mother."

"I love our daughter very much," Harmony said.

Tears rolled down Harmony's cheeks, but because of all the trouble I have put the two of you through, I would be willing to let Rebecca go with whom she chooses, for as long as she chooses."

Rebecca looked at her mother, not knowing what to say.

"Don't worry, Rebecca. If you want to go with your father, you won't hurt mommy's feelings. Being we're in the Military Service and traveling a lot, it would be better for you to have roots."

"What about Hector?" Rebecca asked.

"He goes with us. He is all my responsibility.

Harmony looked at her young daughter, then said, "Do not, for one second, think I am trying to unload you, sweetheart. I would never do that. If you want to come with us, you're more than welcome."

"No, I want to stay with daddy. Besides, you are about to have another child with Peter. With me living with dad, you would have more time for the baby."

"Is that why you want to go with your father?"

"No, I want to be with my brother and sister, like a real family and not travel all over the world."

"Harmony, you and Pete are welcome at our home whenever you want," Sherry told them, "Am I right, Ralph, or Sheldon, which is it?"

"You make the choice of what name you want to call me. I'll come to either."

"Maybe, I will let you keep both names. It will be like being married to two different men at one time. One night I can sleep with Ralph and the other Sheldon."

Everyone laughed.

www.ingramcontent.com/pod-product-compliance
Lightning Source LLC
Chambersburg PA
CBHW061229070526
44584CB00030B/4045